Teachings Around the Sacred Wheel

TEACHINGS AROUND THE SACRED WHEEL

Finding the Soul of the Dreamtime

Lynn V. Andrews

1817

Harper & Row, Publishers, San Francisco

New York, Grand Rapids, Philadelphia, St. Louis
London, Singapore, Sydney, Tokyo, Toronto

I would like to give special acknowledgment to Jack Crimmins for his tireless work and belief in this project, and to Kathy Duckworth for the support and loving care that helped make this workbook possible.

TEACHINGS AROUND THE SACRED WHEEL: *Finding the Soul of the Dreamtime.* Copyright © 1990 by Lynn Andrews Productions, Inc. All rights reserved. Printed in the United States of America. No part of this book may be used or reproduced in any manner whatsoever without written permission except in the case of brief quotations embodied in critical articles and reviews. For information address Harper & Row, Publishers, Inc., 10 East 53rd Street, New York, NY 10022.

FIRST EDITION

Library of Congress Catalogue Card Number 89-45524
ISBN 0-06-250022-8

90 91 92 93 94 VICKS 10 9 8 7 6 5 4 3 2 1

To Agnes Whistling Elk,
Ruby Plenty Chiefs,
the Sisterhood of the Shields,
and the Great Beings of the Dreamtime

Contents

Preface

I am a woman of the twentieth century, a white woman living in an urban setting and in an era in which we have lost our traditions, our ceremonies, our rituals. In losing touch with these ancient circles of mystery, which were once the gateways to uncommon dimensions of reality, we have lost touch with the wilderness of our own spirit.

I write at a time of hope, however. Many of us are reaching out, looking for alternative ways to understand the rhythms of Mother Earth, to worship God or the Goddess, and to balance the male and female energies within ourselves and on the planet. We have come full circle in our quest, and the ancient concepts of shamanism, the sacred Dreamtime, and the sacred wheel of shamanic teaching are now alive and fresh again. We have been able to move around the wheel from shamanism through science and back again to the beginnings, to our origins. We can again realize that we are nothing without the Great Spirit, the Creator; we are nothing without our magnificent Mother Earth, who gave us life. We are made from stars and to the stars we must return.

Throughout my journey, I have been blessed with extraordinary teachers, native teachers, women who have taught me the ancient and sacred way of woman. My teachers, who are called the Sisterhood of the Shields, have taught me that three hundred thousand years ago, the star nations came down to Mother Earth from the Pleiades, and they invested great knowledge in our planet. This knowledge was planted, like seeds, in the oceans, the trees, and the mountains, and this wisdom has been uncovered at various times throughout our history when—but only when—our societies have been ready to hear it.

Much of what was told was memorized by certain women who represented the indigenous cultures of the world. These few women transmitted this wisdom, through the oral tradition, to their daughters and apprentices throughout time until now.

Teachings Around the Sacred Wheel describes some of what I have learned and have been asked to teach by the Sisterhood in my own process of evolving. When I was in Nepal and Tibet, I prepared with the Sisterhood, and then with the help of my research at home in Los Angeles, a series of trainings to be given at certain times. This workbook is the result of that process.

The work here is designed to help beginning shamans exercise their intent, their shaman will, their ability to visualize and manifest on several different levels of consciousness. Every word and sound is chosen carefully to produce an elevating effect within the person using the book. The book is not devoted exclusively to traditional Native American tribal techniques; it incorporates the shamanistic teachings of the Sisterhood of the Shields.

We in the Sisterhood are shamans, but we are not affiliated with any tribe. The teachings that we pass along originated three hundred thousand years ago, but we are of this time and of this soil, and I have learned that we must make peace with the spirits of this land. It has been shown to me that no one owns the truth, that we—as children of Mother Earth—must reach hands across cultural boundaries and heal our Great Mother.

Whether we live in the great cities of the world or in the wilderness, all of us, through the sacred teachings, can learn to reconnect with our origins.

Lynn V. Andrews

Introduction

What is a shaman? What is it that we are really trying to learn? A shaman is someone who understands and learns to choreograph the energies of the universe in order to heal the self and others in a sacred way. The shamanism that I teach is the shamanism memorized and taught by the Sisterhood of the Shields.

The Sisterhood holds up the shield of the firstness of woman. It is an ancient system of knowledge that is oriented to the warrioress or goddess, and that relates to the earth, the stars, and the primal energies of the earth as female.

Today when we look out at the world, we see an ailing Mother Earth that is desperately out of balance. When you look at a system that is out of balance, you have to discover what is missing. You ask yourself, "What would bring this earth back into balance?"

What my teaching is and what this book is about is the manifestation of feminine consciousness. We need to understand the source of power, feminine consciousness, today, to bring the world back into harmony.

This workbook contains a series of visualization techniques to enable apprentices or students to open up their abilities to visualize, to rally their abilities to use and to strengthen their imaginations. You must learn that what you imagine is real. The art of deep trance visualization is an ancient shamanistic technique used for spirit journeys and employing symbols rather than the spoken word. Symbols reach a greater depth and provide shamans with an extraordinary landscape for their work, which would ordinarily be limited by language, culture, and the physical dimension. We begin with words for the sake of communication and move into the powerful realm of each person's individual imagination.

Remember that energy follows thought. If you need to prove this to yourself, lie on your back in a pond or a pool. Lie on your back with your arms outstretched on both sides. Then close your eyes, get into a state of meditation, feel the energy moving throughout your body, and visualize all that energy moving over to your right side. What will happen as you lie on the surface of the water is that you will roll over to the right. You can also do the same to the left, and you will see that energy, in fact, really does follow thought. That's why when people say you are what you think, in a sense, that's true. You are made up of your thought forms. In fact, you actually are a thought form. If you spend your life in negativity, you will become a negative thought form. If you can move your thinking to more positive aspects in life, you will attract more positive things to you. You will become a much more successful and powerful person.

Therefore, a lot of this early work focuses on clearing out negativity and the psychic and emotional debris within your system. This debris has been left there through this lifetime and through the efforts and events of past lifetimes.

This workbook is for beginning shamans, for persons who have grounded themselves in the physical world, who understand that we come into this earth walk choosing to become enlightened and that the moment we get here, enlightenment is the one thing that we are most afraid of. Actually, our mind becomes fearful because enlightenment literally involves formlessness or an ego death. The mind and the ego are the same, but we are immersed in duality and in the illusion that we each possess a separate ego or mind. Part of your work as a shaman is to overcome the illusion of separateness and to unite. The mind is enthroned as king in our lives. The mind is the greatest tool that we have, but it is only a tool, like the hand; it is something that we must have control of. Unfortunately, many of us let the mind be in control of us. Because of that, we think we are our mind, when actually it is the other way around.

This workbook will empower you to use the mind correctly, to make the mind work for you. The minute you talk about becoming enlightened, the mind, which has a keeper, becomes very frightened. All the mind knows is that death means formlessness. Formlessness to the mind means death, not enlightenment. The mind does not want to die because then it would lose its life, and all life wants to survive. You need to teach your mind that you can learn to see reality in a new and different way. This workbook is a step along that path.

How You Can Use This Book

You can successfully use this book alone, but you may find it more helpful to work through the exercises with a partner, with your family, or in a group. However you use the book, you may first wish to tape the meditations and visualization exercises in your own voice so that you will be free to close your eyes and hear the words.

The exercises in this book are designed to be used again and again. Once you are familiar with the contents of the workbook and have gone through it once, feel free to adapt and modify the exercises and worksheets. Every time you use the meditations, you will find subtle changes. Turning the book into a Dreamtime journal and recording your new responses and impressions are good ways to chart your progress and growth over time.

What You Will Need

Drum

Rattle

Chimes

Drumming tapes (e.g., Michael Harner, Mickey Hart)

Meditation music

Smudge stick made of dried sage, cedar, or sweet grass (often available at metaphysical or New Age bookstores) and an abalone shell; a lighter or matches

Five crystals: two small, special crystals that can be carried on your person; three crystals of any size, at least one of which must be single-terminated

Notebook

Tape recorder to record your own voice reading the meditations. (Tapes are available from me, as well. Please use the address at the back of the book to inquire.)

Teachings Around the Sacred Wheel

Chapter 1

Opening Prayer/Meditation

Close your eyes. Let your body begin to relax into the vision and vibration of these words. Let your body deeply relax. Notice any places in your body where you feel tension, and feel free to move, to let the tension go.

Life is a circle. We are each unique and specific people, points on this circle. In using this workbook, you will be forming a bond that will continue, possibly beyond the end of your life. Your work together with the work of others using this book will be to shine your individual uniqueness, to develop tools and ways to help yourself and others shine, while developing and strengthening your circle, the bond that is formed. This circle will radiate out into the world, a strong, sacred wheel made up of many shining crystals, many fine and important human beings, each with a journey, a journey to discover one's own enlightenment and to help heal our Mother Earth.

Imagine yourself at the ocean on the sand before a great sea. See yourself in a circle of many people, all the people whom you love, your circle, each of you joining hands, touching. Don't worry if you do not exactly see this vision; just feel this vision inside you. Now call the powers of all the directions to be with you, to be with you at the edge of a great sea, which *is* where you are now—at the edge of a great sea, the sea of enlightened vision, new insight, the sea of your unknown, wild, unconscious life—a place where earth and water, conscious and unconscious, meet.

At this new place, I call the sacred powers of all directions to be with you now. Banish any energies that wish you ill will. Call the power of Mother Earth, symbolized by the Great Turtle, the slow one, the necessary one, the one who carries us on her shoulders, the earth spirit who teaches us patience, who teaches us to take one step at a time on our journey here, Powers of the Earth, come in! See the turtle in the middle of your circle, here to guide you in your earth learning.

Powers of the South, Sacred Mouse, come into the center of my circle. Sacred Mouse, Teacher of Trust and Innocence, come in. Teach me today to trust, to find again my innocent eyes, my fresh vision, my childlike wonder of the world. Teach me to see what is right in front of my eyes so that I may gather learning, gather trust, gather the power of touching others in gentle, healing ways. Powers of the South, the Mouse, come in!

Powers of the West, place of intuition, looking within, woman place inside all of us, home of the Great Bear, come into my circle here and now. Bear, bear with your sacred task of hibernation, of dreaming, come into my circle in order to teach me better to go inside and listen. Teach me to go inside all the winter of my life, into the darkness, without fear, with excitement, with your great power, Sacred Bear. I pray that I will learn to be quiet, to hear my inner voice, to distinguish my voice of intuition from the false voices of fear, doubt, and indecision. Powers of the West, Sacred Intuition, Sacred Bear, come into my circle now!

Powers of the North, place of storms of wisdom, mountains of knowledge, home of the Buffalo, come in. Come in, Buffalo, to my circle now. Teach me how to give away, to share what I have learned, to nourish others with the bounty of my beings. Teach me to face the cold, to stand alone when I must, to take care of others like a tribe, like a true circle. Buffalo, Sacred Provider, provide me with wisdom, with knowledge, and with the ability to share what I learn. Powers of the North, come into my circle now!

Powers of the East, come into my circle, be in the middle of my life now. East, place of illumination, light, visionary truth, and experience, home of the Eagle, bird that flies highest and sees farthest, come into the center of my circle and teach me now. Teach me how to rise up above my daily vision, my tired eyes, into new vistas of sight. Teach me to take my vision to my Higher Self. Teach me to let the vision of my Higher Self down into my daily mind and revitalize my life. Teach me to prey upon whatever does not feed my Higher Purpose and to rid myself of false paths that do not serve me. Great Bird of Spirit, Sacred Eagle, Powers of the East, come into my circle now!

Powers of the Sky, Great Spirit, fill my circle now with your great light, as I envision my circle surrounded by infinitely bright yellow light. I am enveloped in your great light, touched deep inside by the power of your healing ways. I stand here in the center of my being and call to each of my brothers and sisters to the center of their being. May the Great Spirit, the One Who Carries Us, the True Guide, nourish our circle, allow the powers of the Earth, the south, west, north, and east to shine in and through us, enlightening our circle and teaching us peace, joy, and wisdom.

May all the powers of all directions guide us and keep us! Ho!

Now, once again place your attention on your body, on your breathing. Let your breath be natural; breathe deep into your belly, the center. Now slowly begin to move your limbs, and at your own pace, get ready to return to this room to do the work we have in this book to do. When you are ready, open your eyes.

Welcome!

Chapter 2

The Feeling of the Universe*

Introduction

This meditation has to do with feeling your oneness with all life, helping you get acquainted with the tools at your disposal. At this point, it would be the crystal in your lap. Visualize the universe of stars, feel your relatedness to all life, to Mother Earth. If you are working in a group, feel your relatedness to the group or to your partner. It is particularly important to pull down the energy of the Pleiades into your shaman center so that the star energy becomes part of your shaman energy. Then again you will be working with projecting that energy into a crystal. This takes visualization if you have developed that ability. If you do not yet have the ability to visualize something in its physical form, at least sense it. Do not get confused or discouraged if you cannot see something exactly. Allow yourself to sense or to feel.

Exercise/Meditation

Sit down next to your partner, if working with one or if you are in a group. You can also do this alone. Each pick up one of your crystals, close your eyes, and feel the energy of Mother Earth in the bottoms of your feet. Breathe deeply, consciously relaxing your entire body. Take some time.

As you are now fully relaxed, begin to sense the energy in the room. Feel the presence of others; feel that there is a connecting link between all of us here. Once again, let your breath be your focus. Hold your crystal in your lap.

Let your breathing drop down into your belly. Below your navel, just below, is your center of power. It is called by the martial artists

---

* You can use this before all the others, to relax.

your *Ki* or *Chi* point or your one-point. By us it is called your shaman power center or simply your place of power. Let your attention be centered here at your one-point. Let all your thoughts and feelings be pulled into this place so that you are extremely focused. We are gathering the energy of the whole room and of each other into ourselves. The harnessing of this energy will hold us in good stead in the future.

Breathe deeply. Now as you hold and continue to gather the energy of this room, the energy of the entire group, imagine this energy as a stream of blue light pouring down into your crown *chakra*. Now begin to imagine the energy of Mother Earth. This is golden light filling you from the earth and centering inside you. We have done or will do much work in the Dreamtime of our sacred Mother Earth. Now focus the healing power of Mother Earth inside you, holding the energy of earth in your place of power.

Now I want you to visualize the universe of stars that are above us every evening, those stars that we so often forget about, so often take for granted. Visualize the stars, the energy of the stars. Imagine how strong and powerful their energy must be. Allow that energy to come into you now. Imagine the specific energy of the Pleiades, the sacred seven sisters, the star constellation shaped somewhat like the outline of a diamond or a kite with a tail. The Pleiades are known for their connection with us here on earth. Draw the energy of the Pleiades into you now. We are made from stars, and to the stars we must one day return.

As you begin to imagine all the stars, bring also the sun and the moon into your sacred center by bringing their energy down through the crown of your head, down through the crown *chakra*, and begin to project this energy into the crystal you are holding in your lap.

As you project the energy into the crystal, hold up the crystal in front of you, still with your eyes closed. Imagine and visualize; project a feeling of love and acceptance of yourself into the crystal. Take a few minutes to really let the feeling of self-love and self-acceptance pour into you and into the crystal. Remember, you have the backing of the universe of sun, moon, stars, and our Mother Earth with you now.

Now point the crystal that you are holding toward the person next to you. Using the crystal as your focus and guide, project love, project acceptance, project harmony, project balance into the person next to you. Take a few minutes in silence to focus your energy and attention on this loving task.

Only through holding the power of our own center and then projecting love and acceptance that we have first developed in ourselves, projecting this love and acceptance out into the world, can we begin to change ourselves, our neighbors, and the world for the better. Hold your center. Then radiate your energy outward into the world in the form of white light. See the entire world luminous and pulsating with white light. Take a deep breath, and feel the energy of Mother Earth coming back into your body. Open your eyes as you feel comfortable.

WORKSHEET

Write down in three steps how you felt about projecting your energy into a crystal.

1.

2.

3.

How do you feel about using crystals as tools?

Did the energy of the Pleiades come down to you?
Describe.

Did you see it in a color?
Describe the form.

How did you feel that energy in your system?

How did it affect you?

Chapter 3

The Act of Power

Introduction

As I have mentioned so many times, before you can really begin to build what Agnes calls the Spirit Lodge of your own being, you must look at the foundation of that Spirit Lodge. The foundation has to do with your physical life: how you deal with your environment, how you earn money, how you live with dignity and take care of your children or the people you are responsible for. The foundation of the Spirit Lodge is in essence a paradigm of your totality; your own being must be very secure and very well grounded. When the foundation of your Spirit Lodge is very secure and strong and well executed in life, then I move on in my teaching to what Agnes calls the dome of your lodge. That has to do with spiritual ceremonies and ritual and higher education and higher levels of the other dimensions of reality. If you begin to work with the dome of your Spirit Lodge first, without dealing with the foundation of the lodge, at some point, everything comes toppling down, just like a building falls when the foundation is not secure.

In the beginning work on the foundation of the Spirit Lodge, I talk a lot about the act of power. To be secure in your physical life, you have to know what your destiny is in this lifetime, what your path is. Whether you are working in a group with a teacher or just with yourself, it is important at this point to ask yourself, "What is it that I have a passion about doing in this life?" I often ask people what they would be or who they would be on the cover of *Time* magazine, because being on the cover of *Time* magazine is an example of accomplishing something in the physical plane. If you were on the cover of *Time* magazine, what would the description or the legend underneath your picture read? For me, for example, it would be "Author and Shaman Healer."

I am lucky. All my life I have been a writer and wanted to be a writer. All my life I have wanted to be a healer, and I have been interested in other levels of consciousness and shamanism. So for me to be a shaman healer and a writer is very comfortable. But so often I talk to people who in childhood had a passion or a dream of being a dancer or an artist or maybe a politician, but in fact they become an insurance person or a secretary or the head of a union. They take a path that really has nothing to do with what is in their heart, what they really desire to do. If asked, "If you had it all to do over again, forgetting about whether you're a man or a woman, forgetting about your education and your responsibilities in life, what would you be doing?" almost always they will say, "Oh, I would never be doing this. If I had my druthers, I would rather be a healer" or whatever. So I help that person move along that path because whatever you really want to do you can in fact do.

To find your act of power in this life gives you a point of view. It gives you a starting place where you can get comfortable and successful in your physical life. It is important, whether it's becoming a baker, a housewife, an actress, the president of the country, whatever it is. It requires an extraordinary amount of focus. It demands an extraordinary act of power using all your will to accomplish this act.

I would like to tell you a short story about what my act of power was and is and how it came into being. I was living in Los Angeles, and I had been working with Agnes and Ruby for perhaps three years. At one point, I had been in Canada working with the two of them. I had always wanted to be able to stay on the reserve for longer periods of time. In the first two or three years of our work together, they had asked me to keep my relationship with them very secret, so I told no one except two very, very dear friends about my journeys to Canada. I was always saying that I was going down to Mexico or going to Hawaii or going up north to visit my godparents.

On this particular journey when I was with Agnes, she looked at me one day and said, "Little Wolf, why don't you come and stay with us for a couple of years?"

I was so very excited. It was the first time that Agnes had asked me to spend that much time. She usually kicked me out after a few weeks. So I went home and rented out my house to someone who had me sign an ironclad lease for two years. My daughter was away at school, and I went back up to Canada with two bags. At this point in my life, I had very, very little money. I arrived in the middle of the night, and I came running down the hill to see Agnes doing something very unusual. She was sitting out in front of her cabin before a small fire as if she were waiting for me or someone.

I came down the hill, and I called a greeting to Agnes. I said, "I'm here. I'm here."

She turned around with the coldest eyes I had ever seen and said, "What are you doing here?"

I said, "But, Agnes, you asked me to come live with you for a couple of years. What do you mean what am I doing here?"

She said, "Oh, no. You must have misunderstood me." And that's when she held up her fingers and she said, "It is time. We live in a time of vision. It is time to let the eagles fly. Take what you have learned about the sacred way and power of woman. Take what you have learned in all of our work together to your people."

I said with tears of confusion running down my cheeks, "But, Agnes, you have told me not to tell anyone about our relationship."

She said, "Well, now is the time to change all of that."

I looked at her with astonishment and hurt and anger, totally confused. "How can I do that, Agnes? How can I possibly take what you have taught me to my people? What do you want me to do, stand on a street corner on a soapbox?"

Agnes shook her head and laughed. She said, "No, my daughter, do what you are destined to do. Write the first of many books about our work together, and do not return until the first manuscript is finished. I will never see you again if you do not do this task because we can go no further in our learning together until you have made your act of power."

I was horrified. I started to cry. "Why did you ask me to rent out my house? Why did you ask me to come up here and then turn on me like this? I don't understand, Agnes. I have no money, and I have no place to go."

"That's your problem," she said. "I will see you again when the manuscript is finished."

She would not even let me stay that night. She threw me out. I didn't understand why she had done this. I was so terribly confused. I went back to Los Angeles in a rage. Slowly it began to dawn on me that there was a reason for all this. I knew that I had always wanted to be a writer. I had taken copious notes in journals of everything Agnes or Ruby had ever said to me. I had written everything we had learned together. It was obvious that what I wanted to do was write; yet I had never had the courage, the discipline, the organization to put my work into book form. Agnes knew this about me. She knew that I was undisciplined and unfocused; but if she had told me that, it would have gone in one ear and out the other, not making a bit of difference in my life. I would have agreed with her and gone on doing exactly what I was doing, which was really a lot of nothing when I look back on it. She had seen this in me. She realized that you cannot tell people about themselves, but you have to allow them to have the experience of their own inadequacies.

An act of power provides a mirror. This mirror is one of the best ways, one of the only ways, to learn about yourself. To look in the mirror that you create, yourself, through your own effort and focus, is an extraordinary tool. That is what I am asking of you. I am asking you to find deep in your heart and soul your act of power. It may be difficult for you to do this without working with me on a one-to-one basis, but I think that if you are working with a group or if you can work with a friend, you can delve into the depths of each other's spirits and come up with something very specific and pragmatic. I don't want to hear an act of power that sounds like, "I want to be known as someone who brought love and light into the world." Even though that is a beautiful thought, it is not an act of power. I want to hear something really definite, like a doctor, a lawyer, a homemaker, a gardener, an author— something that you can truly say, "This is my act of power." This is an important task, particularly for some women. It is difficult for many women to develop their outward form in the patriarch world that they live in. It requires taking a stand and being noticed for your power. It is difficult but essential. Then proceeding from that commitment comes a ceremony that I want to give you at this point.

Ceremony

This is an act of power ceremony. It consists, first, of a list called Life Prayer Arrow. The Life Prayer Arrows are actual sticks or arrows you will make. First, make a list of ten things you are going to do by this time next year to make your act of power happen, ten very specific things.

The Death Prayer Arrow consists of a list as long as you want of all the things you are going to give away, that have kept you, all your life, from making your act of power, things like: I'm not good enough, fear of being successful, and so forth. It can be as long as you want.

This is a very helpful ceremony, a ceremony that the Sisterhood and I do at the beginning of every year to keep ourselves focused for that year so we know what we're doing from beginning to end through the twelve months.

When you have your lists written (sometimes it takes a couple of months to get these lists together), make two arrows, one for the life arrow and one for the death arrow. The death arrow must be made out of a flammable material, like a stick, very dry, because you're going to burn it. You will want it to burn easily. Put four streamers on the ends of both sticks: red, white, black, and yellow—little satin ribbons that will represent the four directions. Tie a feather onto each stick. You can paint the sticks, make them beautiful, whatever you'd like to do with them. I usually make them about six inches long, but they can be whatever length you like. Then tie your lists on them, like a scroll wrapped around the arrow.

Then make two small (three or four inches in diameter) spirit of place bundles exactly the same. Wrap the bundles in red, natural material. Red is for the power of woman to protect the energy of what you put in the bundles. Place a little candle in each bundle, some incense (sage, cedar, sweetgrass, or all three), a pinch of cornmeal and tobacco, matches, and a flower or some flower petals. Put these spirit of place bundles in a small blanket that is large enough for you to sit on. I use a red medicine blanket. Take whatever things you would like to have with you in your ceremony. They could be anything—crystals, a personal pipe, whatever you use that means something special in your life, things that give you power, things that make you feel empowered by their presence. Wrap them up in your blanket. I usually roll the blanket up and tie it at both ends with a leather thong. Also include in your blanket a larger pouch of loose tobacco. Of course, include your Life and Death Prayer Arrows.

Go out into the wilderness, where you are not going to be disturbed. Find a hill you can climb, and go to the bottom of this hill. At the bottom of this hill, find a power spot, a place that feels good to you, feels warm to you. Take your loose tobacco and find four stones, which represent the four directions to you.

The south stone represents trust and innocence for the south. The color is red, although the stone does not have to be red. The stones do not have to be any specific color, but just know in your mind that the south is trust and innocence and is represented by the color red.

Find a stone for the west. The color of the west is black. The west stone represents the sacred dream, death and rebirth, transformation. Place a stone in the west of your sacred circle.

Find a stone for the north. The north is the color white, strength and wisdom. Place it in the north.

The find a stone and place it in the east of your sacred circle. The color of the east is gold or yellow. It is the place of the rising sun, the place of illumination and the sacred clown.

After you have placed your stones, take your tobacco and move from the south around to the west, north, and east. Say a prayer as you do this, a prayer for protection. This prayer could be something like, "I place an aura of divine love and protection around this sacred circle so that I am protected from all harm. Ho!" Then enter the circle from the east door, carrying your blanket, and close it behind you by spreading tobacco behind you.

Place your blanket out after you smooth the ground with your hands within your sacred circle, and face south. Then place your death arrow in the ground. The arrow represents the male, and the earth is female; so you have performed a perfect balance. Then take out one of your spirit of place bundles, unwrap it, and light the candle—all you need is a flicker of light. If it doesn't stay lit because of the wind, it is all right. Then light your incense (sage, cedar, or sweetgrass), and smudge the area around you. Smudge yourself, taking the smoke and covering your body with it. Be careful lighting the incense and the candle anywhere in the wilderness. Be very careful about fire. Take special care that nothing dry is around you, that you have smoothed the ground carefully. Smudge all your sacred things that you have laid out on your blanket and the prayer arrows.

At this point, you can sing; you can pray in whatever way is appropriate for you, remembering that this ceremony is for you. So in a sense, it is self-generated. This is not a ritual. This is not something done by rote that must be the same every time you do it. It is a ceremony, so there is something of you in it. It may be a little different for everyone who performs it.

What you are doing with the spirit of place bundle is making an effort to wake up the spirits of place. The spirits of place have been asleep in all the named and nameless things for thousands of years or at least since the last ceremony was done at this particular spot. They are sleeping, and they need to be awakened. To do this, they must see light, and they must hear your voice to know if you are true. You offer them incense as a blessing. This is something beautiful, which is what they love. They love to see flowers and the light from a flame. Offer the spirits of place the flower. Offer tobacco and cornmeal, and start to sing to them. Be sure that you speak out loud. Sing fairly loudly; they need to hear you.

When you hear shamans talk to the spirits of place, calling them to wake up, it is as if they are speaking to a lover. Tell them how beautiful they are. They are little luminous beings who are very curious, and they will begin to wake up. If you are lucky, you will perhaps be able to see them—perhaps an outline of light, perhaps a little shape that's like a cloud. If you cannot see them, you will sense them like air on your skin, very, very subtle. Do not proceed with your ceremony until you sense their presence, even if you do not see them. When finally you feel their presence, thank them for being with you, and then begin your prayers to the Great Spirit.

What I say is,

Great Spirit, Mother Earth, Powers of the Four Directions, my power animal, my allies, my ancestors, and all those who love me, hear me now. This is a ceremony for my act of power. Thank you for being with me. I honor your presence within my circle, my sacred circle. This is my Death Prayer Arrow. These are all the things that have kept me from my act of power all this long time. These are all the things I am willing to give away so that I may accomplish my act of power, my act of destiny in this lifetime. Within this next year, I will begin.

Then read all the things on your list for your death arrow. You can scream them, you can cry them, you can dance them, or you can just simply read them, but say them as if it is an act of will. Use the energy and the power around your solar plexus, and say them with conviction.

Remember that you are making a promise to the Great Spirit. Do not make it lightly. Do not give away something that you cannot truly give away.

When you are finished reading this list to the Great Spirit, burn the arrow and the list, then bury the ashes carefully and completely within the center of the sacred circle. When you are finished, cover it over carefully, putting out any embers. Give thanks to the Great Spirit and the spirits of place. Leave your spirit of place bundle. Wrap up your things, and leave the sacred circle by the east door.

Walk to the top of the hill. At the top of the hill, do exactly the same thing. Find four stones for a sacred circle, a place of power for you, a place of power that feels good, perhaps feels warm to you, and repeat exactly the same ceremony. Placing your life arrow in the ground, forming the balance between the male and the female, open your spirit of place bundle. Perform exactly as you did before. Make your prayer to the Great Spirit, and read, this time, everything on your life arrow. When you are finished reading it, place it again on the arrow. This time leave the arrow to the universe, asking for guidance and asking the universe to help you on your way.

When you are completely through with this ceremony, take note of everything that has happened during the two ceremonies. Take note of what birds have flown over and from what direction. What was happening with the wind? How did the earth feel? What clouds came over and in what configurations? Sense everything. Be totally aware.

When the ceremony is over and you have left your sacred circle by the east door, take your blanket and your sacred things, come down the hill, and celebrate that evening. Have someone take you out to dinner as if you have graduated from college. It is a very important day, really a feast day. If you were living in a tribal situation, you would have a feast, and you would dance. It would be a celebration for you. It should be. You have made a commitment to the Great Spirit, to yourself, and to the universe to make your act of power. You have now truly begun your shaman path. Ho!

WORKSHEET

Life Prayer Arrow List

1.

2.

3.

4.

5.

6.

7.

8.

9

10.

Death Prayer Arrow List (As Long as You Want)

Describe what was happening during your ceremonies. What was happening with the wind? How did the earth feel? What birds flew over from what directions? Describe everything that you were aware of.

It is good to have a vision, a dream.
  —Agnes Whistling Elk

We are all one, standing in your light, Great Spirit,
your light like the golden sun.
I give thanks.
  —Ruby Plenty Chiefs

Chapter 4

Balancing

Introduction

The balancing exercise is to be done with a partner in a group or just with a partner alone. This is an exercise that is located on the south on the sacred wheel. It should be done with trust and innocence. It is an exercise designed to expand and exercise your ability to visualize and to send out and to receive energy. Both are equally important—to send out and receive the energy of Mother Earth and the feeling of expansion and love that is needed for true success in shamanistic work. This exercise is also to help you experience the feeling of the shaman power center around your navel.

Exercise/Meditation

Please turn to your partner or the person on your right if you are working in a group and ask permission to do with him or her a meditation on joy. Introduce yourselves, and talk to each other for a few moments.

Stand up and turn to face each other. Hold your hands up with palms facing each other. Then rub your own hands together fast and hard for a moment. Now blow your breath over your palms. Your palms should tingle. Always remember that breath is of the spirit and that by blowing your breath on your palms, you are balancing the essence of the spirit with your physical body. Now reach out to your partner and hold your palms an inch away from his or her palms. Close your eyes, breathe deeply, and be sure your spine is perpendicular to the floor. Be receptive to your partner and still your mind completely. Visualize greenish white light surrounding your heart. Take a deep breath; then, with love, project that radiant light into your partner's heart. Feel your whole body expand and relax as you open your being in trust and innocence to the life-giving force of your partner. Keep your shoulders back, and continue to send love for a few moments.

Now visualize golden light surrounding you, enveloping your partner and finally radiating out and circulating around the room to the right. Take a deep breath, and place your feet a little apart, bending your knees slightly. Visualize yourself as a giant redwood tree. Feel your feet on the floor, and then feel your roots extending deep down into the earth below you. Take another deep breath as you feel the sacred energy of Mother Earth moving up through your roots into your tall trunk. Feel how securely you are rooted into the earth and how strong, proud, and straight your trunk feels. Now lift up your arms as you feel the earth's life force spreading out through your healthy, strong branches. Now gently squat down a foot or so, and with your arms stretched, still above your head, very gently imagining that there is a gentle warm wind, begin to sway back and forth in the breeze, back and forth, back and forth.

Lower your arms and straighten up. Take a deep breath, and slowly open up your eyes, feeling your groundedness.

Now one of you pick up two of your crystals and face your partner. There is not a person here who is not capable of doing this next exercise. Working one at a time, take the crystal in your right hand and place it on the left foot of your partner, holding it there. Think of femaleness, woman, and what it means to be feminine. Whether you're working on a man or a woman, the left side is female. Slowly move the crystal up your partner's left side; you will feel a tingling sensation as these crystals move up to the top of the head. Now, moving it back down, let it settle on the spot that feels sticky or most a place of feminine power. That could be anywhere: elbow, ankle, or wherever. Then let your partner hold the crystal on that spot while you do the same thing on his or her right side with the crystal in your left hand. This time you are looking for the spot that is most a place of masculine power.

When you find it, let your partner hold the crystal there. Now take a deep breath. Those holding crystals close your eyes and visualize your balanced sense of power in your navel area surrounded by pink light. Then with your will and force of power, think about the balance of male and female energies within your body. Using the power of your will, see your male and female energies symbolized by the two crystals, and slowly bring them together and balanced over your navel.

Take a deep breath, and remember what it feels like to have these energies balanced and your being grounded.

Now open your eyes and repeat the exercise on your partner, starting again with your right crystal on your partner's left side.

WORKSHEET

Write a brief paragraph discussing how you felt about your energy center, your shaman center.

How did it make you feel to receive energy, light, and love from and give them to another person?

Where on your body did you find the masculine and feminine places of power? Describe.

Chapter 5

Up the Mountain

Introduction

This meditation has to do with giving away emotional, psychic, and intellectual debris within your system. The sacred mountain is a mountain that you walk up in a spiraling fashion. At certain levels along the way, you give away forever, hopefully, things that have been keeping you back from reaching within yourself the summit of your sacred mountain, the sacred mountain that represents your path to enlightenment and spirit in life.

If your cup of life is full, if you have collected so many assumptions and judgments and feelings and things that limit your consciousness in life, you need the opportunity to give them away, to search them out, and to give them up so you may grow further. It is important to have an empty cup, to begin with, in your shaman journey. You can move on and fill that cup with more useful things.

It would be a good idea to do the up the mountain meditation once a month with your family or friends, with people you work with, certainly with yourself. It is a wonderful exercise to practice with your family to promote communication. Lots of times we carry emotional and intellectual baggage that we don't even know we have. In a deep state of meditation, we can more easily find these things and declare them to the Great Spirit.

If you are working in a group, when you are finished with this meditation, discuss everything you have found. Be sure you use the worksheet pages provided just for this work, that you write down everything you find during this and the other meditations so you can go back over it. Every year you will find you have different things to give away. It's good to have all these things written down so you can see how far you have come.

Exercise/Meditation

In doing this first meditation, you will be learning to exercise your shaman will. Pick up three of your crystals that feel to be of similar power and weight. Sit with your shoulders back and square and your spine perpendicular to the floor, and hold one crystal to your navel. Breathe deeply, visualize a yellow, golden light, and sense its strength. Then concentrate on your own power, and send that light and energy into your crystal. Take a moment to do this.

Now set that crystal in front of you.

Pick up the other two crystals, and realize how holding a crystal in each hand polarizes your male and female energies. Breathe deeply, and experience how different these forces are. First concentrate on the crystal in your right hand. Feel its energy tingling up through your hand and arm and into your body. Examine the masculine nature of its energy. Now hold that crystal to your throat *chakra*, and visualize a beautiful sky blue color entering the crystal. Tense your solar plexus, and will this to be so. I'll give you a few minutes.

Now place that crystal by your right side. Visualize it glowing with blue light.

Now take the crystal in your left hand, and sense it increasing your feminine power. Feel its strength tingling up through your palm and into your arm. Feel how the crystal enhances your female power. Take a deep breath, and allow yourself to explore this feeling.

Now hold this crystal to your heart, and visualize the color green, like a beautiful field of green alfalfa or a rolling lawn. Breathe several deep breaths through your nose. Tense your solar plexus; then with a strong breath through your mouth, will the color green and the expanding sense of love to enter the crystal. Feel your heart open and flood with an overwhelming feeling of love. Let this love enter the crystal on a beam of green light. Now place the crystal on the floor on your left side. Take a deep breath, and center yourself between the two crystals on either side. Take a moment.

Now pick up the crystal in front of you with both hands. Hold it to your third eye or shaman eye. Feel its coolness on your forehead. Take a deep breath, and realize that holding a crystal with both hands balances your male and female energies. This balancing helps open your *chakra* centers to a clear flow of energy. Take a moment to see this energy flowing freely up from your feet, throughout your body, up to your crown *chakra*, and spiraling back down through your system. A good way to visualize this is to feel the energy coarsing up your right side in the color blue and, at the top of your head, transforming to green and running down your left side and transforming again to blue at your feet. Try running this energy flow for a few minutes. Remember to breathe deeply through your nose as you do this, centering yourself.

Now feel the balanced energy in your body, and begin to sense how your own vibrating harmonizes perfectly with the vibration of the crystal in your hand.

Whenever you have an emotion or thought that you want to be rid of, do this exercise using a single terminated crystal, or what is called a shooter crystal. Hold it on your solar plexus, visualizing gold light, and point it toward the ground. Concentrate on the unwanted emotions, and blowing out through your mouth, flood the crystal with your negative thoughts. Do this for several minutes or until you feel a sense of relief. The crystal may become dark and cloudy. Now, still pointing the crystal toward the ground, with the force of your will and with your solar plexus tensed, send all unwanted thoughts and emotions into the floor and through to the ground. See this happening through the tip of the crystal, like a brown, muddy river pouring into a deep crevice in the earth and being absorbed by the earth until it totally disappears. Take a moment. When it is all gone, take a deep breath through your nose and relax. If you do this outside, you can also bury the crystal, or you can take it home and place it in sea salt water for four days to clear it.

For now, I want you to remember this exercise. Leaving the three crystals where they are, I want you to lie down, with a crystal at your feet and one on each side.

Take several deep breaths and clear your thoughts.

Imagine that it is a beautiful summer day and you are walking next to a small stream that winds its way across a green valley. You smell the flowers and the earth. A warm breeze caresses your skin. Up ahead you see a beautiful mountain jutting up out of the valley floor. You are drawn to this mountain in some inexplicable way from deep inside of you. Your pace quickens with anticipation.

Let your breath be natural. Breathe into the center of your being, relax. You enjoy this wilderness place. It feels good to you. It is a place of power. See yourself facing the large mountain. It's okay if you don't visualize the mountain exactly. Feel the mountain or sense it. You don't have to have a perfect picture. You know you are going to journey up this sacred mountain.

Continue to let your breath be in the center of your being. Breath is light; it is a source of energy. Imagine standing at the base of the mountain and looking up. This is your mountain, the mountain of your life. It symbolizes your journey to enlightenment. You watch the clouds above in the turquoise blue sky. Take a moment in silence to give thanks. Give thanks to yourself, to the work and love that you share in this world.

Now you feel ready to begin your journey. But first you must prepare for the long climb by lightening your load. Sit down in the grass under a tree and ask yourself what you need to leave behind in terms of your physical self, your physical nature, or your physical attachments in order to undertake the journey up this sacred mountain. Take a minute in silence to discover what you need to leave behind physically or materially, and enact a small ceremony like the one you just did with the shooter crystal, saying to yourself, "I now leave this behind in order to continue to grow, to know myself in my true nature, and to seek enlightenment." Put these thoughts into the crystal, and shoot them into the ground until they disappear.

Now begin to walk up the mountain on a winding trail. The view below is very beautiful as you begin to climb. You feel the dirt under your feet as the path becomes steeper. You are walking on a spiraling trail that winds around the mountain all the way to the top. Already you are becoming a little tired. You come to a place a quarter of the way to the top. There is a flat area where you can sit. Draw a circle in the dirt with your hand, and sit within this sacred wheel. Ask yourself, "What do I have to let go of *emotionally* in order to continue my journey to enlightenment?" Trust your intuitive voices to help you, and listen to the answers that come. Enact a simple ceremony of letting go with your crystal, stating that you will let go and you will remember what you have left behind. Take a few minutes in silence to do this. Breathe deeply.

Now continue walking. The trail is even steeper now, and you begin to struggle to keep up a good pace. But you feel clearer inside yourself. You keep walking, though it is difficult, until you get halfway up the trail. You come to a place where there is a large boulder. You feel this is a good place to rest. You choose to sit with your back to this boulder. Feel the cool stone, the solidity, the power of this rock. Look out into the distance. See the beautiful valley below and the tiny stream like a silver ribbon. As yourself, "What do I need to let go of *intellectually* in order to continue my journey of self-exploration? What blocks do I have in this area?" Let the silence be your guide, as breath is your guide, on the path of releasing old fears, worries, whatever is necessary for you to let go of. Take a few minutes in silence, and see yourself letting go, physically removing all blocks that occur on the intellectual level that keep you from your own enlightenment. Place them in the crystal, and shoot them into the ground.

Now walk again, feeling rested and paying attention to every step, because the trail is narrow and very steep. Journey in greater and greater confidence and joy until you reach a place just below the peak of the mountain. There is a rock ledge where you can rest and dangle your feet over the valley far below. See yourself sitting on this ledge. There is ample room, but none to spare. Ask yourself this question, letting the powers that be, inside you, around you, come forward to answer: "What do I need to let go of *spiritually* in order to stand fully atop my mountain?" Listen in silence, remember, and enact a ceremony of letting go again, using your crystal. Finally, you feel a sense of joy and release. You stand up, back away from the ledge, and realize that your head is so high it is almost in the clouds that surround the top of the mountain. With eager anticipation, you scramble up the trail.

You are now standing on the top of your mountain. Look around in all directions. You watch an eagle high in flight. The air is colder up here—very brisk. The trees look like tiny sticks on the valley floor. Know that this is the mountain of your life. This is also the mountain of every day. You climb this mountain every day whether you know it or not. I encourage you to know, fully know, that you are on this path, this journey of the sacred mountain. Look around at the ground here. There are pieces of mica, sparkling in the sunlight. Notice the blue flowers. Touch them. Be aware of everything—the clean air and the evergreen trees around you. Then see on the ground a crystal, a very special crystal, a crystal of light, of beauty unlike any you have ever seen before. Pick up the crystal, and hold it to your heart and then up to the light.

See its rainbow colors. Let the rays of the sun enter the crystal. As you hold the crystal, I want you to hear a prayer forming in your heart. This is your prayer for harmony.

Trust what words come.

Trust harmony.

Trust balance.

Trust that you will remember what is necessary to let go of.

Slowly begin your walk down the mountain, repeating your prayer in the silence in your heart. Your walk down the spiraling trail is much easier. You hold your beautiful new crystal with joy, knowing that it marks the top of the mountain. As you pass each area where you rested and gave away, you touch the crystal to your heart and give thanks.

As you reach the lower part of the mountain, you look out over the lengthening shadows that lace the floor of the valley. You watch the sun steadily lowering behind the horizon line. Now you are eager to get home before dark. When you have reached the flat ground, let your focus be on your body. Take several deep breaths and, at your own pace, open your eyes.

WORKSHEET

What did you let go of physically? How did it make you feel?

What did you let go of emotionally? How did this make you feel?

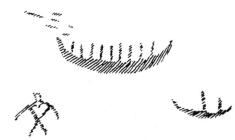

What did you release intellectually? How did it make you feel?

What did you let go of spiritually? How did it make you feel?

Sisterhood of the Shields,
I send my deepest gratitude to you,
and to all of the beings who help us to live.
You are my counsel and my sacred circle.
I send you energy and light,
and I honor you through all the days of my life.
Ho!

— Lynn Andrews

Chapter 6

The Power Animal Journey

Introduction

You need a rattle and a drum for this journey. This process has been discussed well by Michael Harner in *The Way of the Shaman*.

For the Sisterhood of the Shields, knowing your power animal is essential because the power animal protects and guides you in your work as a healer and a shaman. It helps to do this meditation with a partner or a group, but you can do it alone. At the end of the journey, blow the spirit of your animal into the palms of your hands, quickly hold your palms and your breath over your navel area, and then dance your animal.

Finding your power animal enables you to travel for the first time into the Lower World, home of the ancestors and the power animals. It is important to experience the spiraling tunnel that leads you there and to learn to feel at home in the often mysterious landscape.

Fast for at least one day before attempting this journey.

Exercise/Meditation

Lie down, close your eyes, take several deep breaths, and move deeply into a state of meditation. This is not meant to be a frightening journey. I want you to realize in your deepest self—that part of yourself that wants to become all knowing and wise and a shaman—that this journey we are about to go on is a journey back into your own primordial time, back into your own history as an intelligent human being. We are searching for your original nature, your power animal.

To find your original nature, we have to begin to uncover your real self. Within your true self dwells your power. It is this power that we need to discover. We are going to travel back (down) into time to your beginnings.

During this dream, I want you to become aware, first of all, of your physical being—your skin, your flesh, your organs, your intestines, and the armature of your skeleton, your bones. Try and feel them. Take a moment to experience your stomach as distinct from your intestines. Feel the fullness or emptiness of your stomach. Feel the energy movement in your intestines. Now feel your heart beating. Now take a deep breath, and sense the expansion of your lungs. Feel your ribs moving.

Now tense your leg muscles, and feel the muscles held in place by your leg bones. Realize how perfectly your body functions and how much you take it for granted. Realize how your organs and glands feed your flesh and clean your blood without your even thinking about it.

Now I want you to let your consciousness wander through your body looking for your true self—that sacred place of power—your original nature. Take your time and, when you find it, remember it. You have come to power because you desire to see. Let power help you. Through the process of mind, we are going to journey into the Lower World, a place that has a great shamanistic value. I am going to provide you with the opportunity to experience your own transformation into what we call "original spirit nature" or your power animal form.

Your power animal is a force of energy that equates with your own primary nature. Your power animal could be a mammal, bird, fish, dolphin, even a dragon; but it is not ever a fanged creature that bares its teeth, a member of the snake family, or any of the creepy-crawlies. If one of those beings presents itself to you in an ominous manner, turn away and go on. If it persists, simply come back up the tunnel and end the journey. Wait and take the journey another time. Let your thoughts clear.

Take another deep breath, and slowly relax your muscles completely. Let your thoughts empty out of your mind. Roll your eyes up in your head, and visualize golden white light emanating from your crown *chakra* at the top of your head. Breathe deeply, and rest in the golden light for a few moments, letting it surround you with its healing protection.

Now imagine that you are walking across a grassy meadow. The grass is green and fragrant, and there are red and yellow flowers blooming everywhere. You stop for a moment to smell them. Then you walk on, feeling carefree and happy. It is noon and the sun is high. The temperature is pleasant, and the soft breeze feels like silk on your skin. Be aware of the sounds of life around you. There are prairie dogs scampering into holes. You smell the sweetgrass on the gentle breeze. It is early summer.

You are delighted to see up ahead a pond shimmering in the sunlight like liquid silver. When you reach its banks, you look around and realize that you are completely alone. There is no one for miles. Deciding to take a swim, you strip off your clothes and step into the water. It is warm and clear. As you begin to swim, you dive beneath the surface. With astonishment, you realize that you can breathe under water. You swim around like a porpoise—with great ease. Then you see an opening at the bottom of the pond. A surge of excitement runs through your body as you recognize the opening as the entrance to a spiraling tunnel. You know that this tunnel is a sacred *see-pa-poo*, or the entrance to the Lower World, the home of the power animals. At this point, you remember that after you journey down the tunnel, which is of a very comfortable width, you will come out on a grassy plain. There you will see many birds and animals, but only the one that presents itself to you from four different sides is your power animal. When that happens, approach your animal, and put your arms around it. If you are working with a partner, remember that when you do this, you physically cross your arms over your chest so that your partner knows where you are. Then you bring your power animal back up the spiraling tunnel with you and rest on the shore of the pond. Remember that when you reach the edge of the pond, you should physically sit up. Remember this: As you swim in the pond, something inside of you is irresistibly drawn to the spiral tunnel. You long to discover your power animal, so you head for the tunnel. Very comfortably and easily, you swim down and down in a spiraling fashion toward the Lower World. And now as power speaks to the spirits, your partner will continue to drum and move into your sacred journey.

Blessed beings of the Lower World
Come to us and show your sacred four Directions.
Spirit Beings that protect and empower us—
See our humbleness and hear the sound of our own
    beating hearts.
Ho, sacred Mother and Father Sky—Help us.

Keeping your eyes closed, open your palms in front of your face. Take a deep breath, blow your breath onto your palms, and then quickly press them over your solar plexus and navel. Know that breath is spirit and the spirit of your power animal is within you now to protect and guide you for as long as you live. If you are alone, dance your power animal until it becomes a part of your being. If you are working with a partner, honor the four directions with your rattle and begin dancing your power animal with your partner drumming. Exchange drumming for each other.

If you are in a group, please stand. Where you stand, each of you hold up your rattles and shake them four times facing each of the four directions. Do this now. Then begin to dance your power animal. Your dancing honors that power and makes it even more a part of your being.

Ho!

Honor the new sense of personal power within you.

WORKSHEET

Describe your power animal.

How did the power animal make you feel?

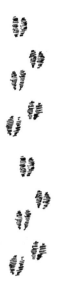

How did the power animal feel about you?

Do some research on your power animal and write down all the attributes of, say, a bear, if you found a bear as your power animal—the bear's feeding habits, when it hibernates, and so forth. You do this so you will have an intimate knowledge of the nature of your power animal.

Chapter 7

Power Animal in a Crystal

Introduction

This visualization is powerful and important because your power animal should be with you at all times. For many of us, it is easier to understand having an intangible being inside a tangible object. For instance, when you are going to a meeting that is very important and you want to be powerful, it helps you to be able to take out a crystal that shines in the light, see prisms of light and rainbows within it, and remember that you have done a sacred ceremony and have worked very hard to make sure your power animal has found an environment that pleases it and that it lives within this crystal. So when you need your power animal at a time when you can't do a ceremony or go out into the desert, mountains, or wilderness or don't have the opportunity to smoke your pipe or can't sit in a sacred wheel or be in a sacred way, it is very important to have this crystal with you. It gives you strength and power. It gives you something tangible to feel with your hand and to look at. It is beautiful. It reminds you of the beauty of your spirit path. It reminds you when the light hits it that there is a meaning to life, that there is a reason that we suffer and live.

Select a beautiful quartz crystal for your power animal so it will be happy within it and will not feel the need to look for another place to live. Consider when you pick this crystal whether you want to wear it around your neck, carry it in your pocket, or put it on your altar at home or in a medicine bag. The size is important, obviously, if you want to carry it with you at important times when you particularly need the power of your power animal. Remember that the power animal is always with you, and when you think of it, you are giving it energy. When you pay no attention to your power animal at times, it can leave you. That is not a good thing because then you are more open to illness and problems in your life. The power animal empowers you.

That's why it is important to remember this crystal. Touch it every day if you don't carry it on you at all times.

Exercise/Meditation

Pick out the crystal that you want as a home for your power animal. Remember this is a crystal that will be in your sacred bundle and will never be used for anything else.

Lie down and close your eyes. Take a deep breath, and totally relax your entire body. As you know, one of the things you are doing in this work is clearing out old energy blockages or psychic debris that is preventing new and higher energy from circulating effectively within your power centers. To help facilitate this process, take another deep breath, and visualize a globe of radiant golden light like the sun. See this sun glowing at the bottoms of your feet. Feel its warmth. This sun is extraordinarily radiant and very, very bright, but it does not burn you. Now visualize this sun moving through and into the soles of your feet. Feel the warmth radiating out toward your toes, and as if you were lying at the beach without a care in the world, feel your body relax. The sun with its brilliant light begins to move up through your feet as you relax your arches. Now it moves slowly up into your ankles. As you relax all those tiny muscles, you see something extraordinary begin to happen. Any psychic debris that has been stored in your joints or your muscles—old memories or old emotions that you hold in your body—simply sparkles and burns like a sparkler on the Fourth of July. You may not have realized before that you were holding this old stuff. But with the help of this bright sun, such debris burns up and disappears.

Now relax your legs completely as the sphere of light slowly moves up your calves and into your knees. If you have held any fear of death, it will be lodged there. See it sparkle and burn away. Still feel the radiant power and warmth of the sun now moving slowly up your thighs and into your pelvic area. See any sexual problems or memories fizzle and burn away. Completely relax, and let go of anything you have been holding onto.

Experience the radiant sun moving up from your hips and into your lower stomach. Take a deep breath and sense your deepening relaxation. Allow old sadness from childhood and disillusionments to burn away as the sun moves up through your stomach. Permit old angers, resentments, or any sense of darkness to disappear as it burns away. As the glowing sun moves up into your solar plexus, completely relax and give away any feelings of powerlessness to the fire.

Consciously relax your chest and back areas as you see and feel the sun slowly moving up the trunk of your body. Feel the warmth as it progresses up through your fingers and hands and arms. Then it moves up through your heart and into your shoulders. Take a few moments to sense the whole lower part of your body and enjoy its new feeling of lightness and relaxation. You breathe deeply, enjoying a new sense of clarity and clearness.

Now bring the fiery disc up into your throat and swallow once, hard. Know that any unspoken problems will be found, and watch them burn away. Completely relax your facial muscles, the muscles around your mouth, jaw, and eyes. Totally relax your forehead and scalp as you relax in the powerful warmth of the sun. And finally, bring the sun up and out through the top of your head. Feel a new sense of lightness and radiant warmth throughout your entire system.

Now you are ready to hold the crystal you are going to use for your power animal to your heart and will these good, clear feelings into the crystal. Visualize a shaft of green light moving from your heart and into the center of the crystal. Take a moment to do this, knowing that you are preparing a loving environment for your power animal. Breathe deeply as you do this. Now move your crystal to your solar plexus area near your navel, your power center. Press it gently into yourself, feeling a sense of warmth as you press.

This is the last time you will touch the crystal until the end of the meditation. When I ask you to pick up the crystal in the Dreamtime, I mean its exact spirit counterpart. Take a deep breath and go even deeper. Bring your consciousness down into your solar plexus. Feel the warmth and power there. Look around for your place of power, an area of well-being within you. When you find that area, smooth it with your spirit hands. Visualize a beautiful red medicine blanket. See it, touch it, feel its fibers. Lay it down on your place of power. Now sit on the red medicine blanket. Get comfortable, place a sacred personal pipe in front of you, sing your power song to yourself, and call for your power animal. See him as a dot on the horizon. See him coming closer and closer until finally he is sitting in front of you in a respectful posture. Look him in the eyes. Take several minutes as you commune together.

Feel the animal's power coming into you. Feel his strength and wonderful sense of peace and well-being. There is golden light surrounding you. Between you, place your power animal crystal. Honor your power animal. I will give you some time to tell your power animal what you want and need from him. He provides protection against illnesses. Tell him your feelings and what it means to you to have his presence in your life. Then allow your power animal to express himself to you and let him tell you how it will empower you. You won't see the animal speak, but if you sit in the center of your interior silence, you will sense the meaning. Take several minutes.

Pick up the crystal and hold it first to the third eye of your power animal. Allow and see the essence of that power animal permeating the entire crystal, and finally see your power animal disappear and reappear inside the crystal. Take a few minutes.

See your power animal inside, surrounded by its natural habitat. Take a few minutes to see the environment in detail. Smell the grass and trees and the earth.

Now place the crystal on your own third eye. See through your third eye to your power animal inside the crystal. See him happy, free, and completely at ease. Know that your power animal will be retained in the crystal forever. Anytime you need to work with him, bring out the crystal. Know that the crystal and you have the same kind of electrical energy. What is inside the crystal is inside you. Wrap the crystal in natural red material. Keep it near you always. This power animal crystal lives in your power center, your solar plexus. Whenever you need to communicate with your power animal, bring your consciousness down into your solar plexus area, spread your medicine blanket, and repeat the Dreamtime ceremony you have just done.

As you take a deep breath, leave your solar plexus and bring your consciousness back up to the top of your head. Begin to feel life force coming back into your body. Take several deep breaths. Feel the energy of Mother Earth coming up into your feet. Take another breath as the life force spirals up your spine and through your entire body. Wiggle your fingers and toes, and slowly open your eyes. Take your time.

Now is the time to take your crystal off your solar plexus, blow

your breath into it, and wrap it in red natural material. If you have
nothing to wrap it in, until you find some red material, place it in a
pocket, purse, or somewhere it will be at rest until you use it again.

WORKSHEET

Describe the environment that you created within the crystal.

Describe what the animal felt like when it was moving into the crystal.

How did you feel about the exercise with the sun moving up through
your system and burning out all your psychic debris?

Did that work effectively for you?

What did you burn up on the way through the *chakra* system in your body?

What feelings did you find that needed to be given away?

Remember each phase of the cleansing exercise clearly, starting with the bottoms of your feet and working up to the top of your head. Then ask yourself what value this cleansing exercise had for your life.

What is the most important thing that happened?

If you felt blocked with this exercise, describe where you felt blocked.

Power Song

Create a power song to call your tutelary spirits, your ancestors, your power animal, or any of the
other beings you work with in the Dreamtime. Your
power song can be simply several lines of "I Am, I
Am, I Am." Or it can be short poem in song form.
It can be written in any way that is meaningful and
powerful for you. It must be expressive of the
essence, soul, and power of your being and must be
easy to remember.

Chapter 8

Dingo Man Dreaming

Introduction

This meditation is about what we choose not to look at in life, the shadow self. The part of us that we do not look at is the part that most likely rules our life. We need knowledge of our own shadow and darkness so we can integrate what we have denied and disowned into our everyday lives. The darkness has been trying to get our attention in many different ways throughout our lifetime. This meditation will help you to see the parts that you have denied.

An aboriginal sand painting is a microcosm of life and all of its experiences. In this meditation, the dingo, like a coyote, is the spirit helper of the Sky Being, Oruncha, who is ageless but ancient, with curly, wild, black hair and a red band around his head. Each of you will experience him in your own way.

Be aware that the dingo is kind. He does not sleep on the sand painting, your sand painting. If you consider most people, they behave like dogs. They run madly into the painting of your life, throwing your colored sands of time out into space, where they can never be found again. You become a victim of their process, and you seem to forget totally that you were creating a painting of your own. The worst thing is that we often step into another's sand painting as if it were our own. And we leave our beautiful designs to scatter to the four winds, unattended.

There is a group of people in Australia who live near the water. They just spend their lives looking into it like a mirror. They are the Half People, and they are split right down the middle. When they hear you coming, they put their halves together and run and hide behind the trees. Most people trade goods and services with each other. The Half People trade only for tobacco. Tobacco is sacred, and its smoke carries messages to the sky beings in the Dreamtime. They hope the Great Spirit will make them whole again. They don't realize that we all must participate in our healing more fully than simply offering tobacco.

Most of us are often like the Half People. When we hear footsteps of other people coming, we put both our sides together and think that our split is invisible and that we look like everybody else. To help us with our incompleteness, we are going to meet an ally. This ally is dark and very powerful. He sees you; he sees each of us. Remember that the dark is the repressed side of our instinctual nature. It is not the devil.

Each person here has been calling this dingo, this ally of darkness with their own fear. There are many things that people choose not to look at in life. And it's what you choose not to see that will eventually rule your life.

What we each need to balance the light in our life is knowledge of shadow and darkness, so that shadow and darkness do not overtake us. In a very true way, shadow and darkness have been trying to get our attention in order to help us. The wonderful light that each person is needs a distinct darkness to define it. The darkness providing your balance and cosmic equilibrium is now only a vague shadow. By witnessing true darkness, the opposite of the goodness that you are, your spirit will become more clearly defined. You will become more fully aware of when darkness or negativity has come into your life, and you will be able to acknowledge it, change it, or leave the situations, instead of simply becoming entangled or lost in the darkness.

One way we do this is to confront the ally, to confront dingo man dreaming. We will call for him. When we do, stay in the protective sphere of your sand painting by staying on the edge, touching the sand painting. No harm will come to you. You are fully protected by the Dreamtime.

Exercise/Meditation

Take several deep breaths, clear your thoughts, and go even deeper. Feel the energy of Mother Earth in the bottoms of your feet. Consciously relax your entire body. Breathe deeply.

Now that you are relaxed, see yourself in a wilderness place—in a clearing of dirt, red sand, and near many trees. Smell the eucalyptus.

Feel the sense of well-being that you feel here.

Trust yourself the more you are entering the Dreamtime. Trust that you are entering into a deeper relationship with your spirit.

Allow yourself to feel the small sure light that emanates from below your navel. Here is your place of power, your center, your place of wellness and beauty.

As you look inside you, notice the crystals that have been placed inside your body and give thanks for this. All is well, and you are safe in body and spirit as you enter and live in the Dreamtime.

We are going to experience the power of dingo man dreaming.

Take a few minutes in silence to simply breathe and become acclimated to silence and the Dreamtime and see your sand painting as clearly as you can.

Now notice that your sand painting is in one area of your wilderness place. Go there and sit before it.

Meditate. See in your mind's eye the shape of spirals and dots in the painting. Take a moment.

Notice near the sand painting that there is a place that looks like an animal has lain down. You realize that here was the bed of a spirit animal, a dingo, which is much like a wild dog or coyote.

Notice your feelings as you look at the impression of the animal's resting place in the sand. Notice by the size of the impression and the shape you imagine that the dingo had eaten well and that his belly was full of food and water. Notice that the dingo has left no footprints in the soft sand.

This dingo has left a map for you in the spirit world. Do not trouble yourself with how a spirit animal that leaves no footprints can leave a trace of his body when he wants to get a message to you; trust that it is so.

As you look at the impression the dingo has left in the earth, begin to see that the impression looks like a cloud and that its legs spread out and down look like a symbol for rain.

Realize that this is the mark of a sky being, an ally. A rain cloud is female and gives birth to life-giving rain.

Now in your sacred Dreamtime wilderness place, go and find ten large stones and bring them to the sand painting. Pile them there to be used in a moment.

Now go and gather some leaves and branches from a cherry tree that you surprisingly find nearby. Smell the fragrant green leaves and pink blossoms. Place them near the stones, and build them into a small fire. Light the fire. It burns easily.

There is a sacred place where the Sky Beings of the Rainbow Serpent meet with the guardians of their children, who still walk the earth. It is a place where no evil can live, and no evil spirit would ever dare to go there. It is a land where there is no sickness, and the great ones live free. There is a lake there where the dolphins swim. It is made of silver shadows, and in the middle grows a native cherry tree. The cherry branches and leaves you have brought represent this center tree. We all burn them, and the smoke carries you deeper into the Dreamtime world. The branches are a gift from Oruncha of Chauritzi, the sacred Sky Being. Sit for a few moments and allow the smoke to envelop you. Breathe in its pungent, refreshing smell. Feel your power.

Now stand up and place the stones evenly on the perimeter of the sand painting. Feel each stone carefully, in each of the four directions and points in between, realizing each stone is different in density and color and has a life of its own.

Now see near you some red ochre earth. Take this earth, and mix it with water in a small pot. Now take off your clothes. Placing both hands in the red ochre, paint your body. Rub it all over you. Feel the smoothness of the ochre and sense how it dries quickly. The red paint makes your body look beautiful. Take a moment as you paint yourself.

Sit down and silently say a prayer of thanks, a prayer of thanks for the good work you are doing.

Now I will enter your Dreamtime space, your wilderness place to help you. See me. I am also covered with red ochre. We embrace each other in the spirit world. Together we put more branches on the fire. Notice in the silence how carefully and well we work together.

The fire is built right next to the sand painting. As we build the fire higher, the wind comes up. It sounds strong, like a bull roarer, whistling and blowing twisters in the sand.

Now I sit opposite you on the other side of the sand painting. Notice now in your mind's eye that, with the fire, the stones, and the sand painting, plus the protective cherry branches next to you, we have many symbols of light. Begin softly, in your imagination, to sing a chant, your power song. Do this silently. Your power song is the way to call the dingo.

Soon you notice dingo footprints, like coyote prints, appearing around the sand painting circle. Then what appears to be the tail end of a dingo appears. Notice it is silvery with a blue tinge. Slowly, as if walking on clouds, the dingo begins to circle the sand painting, its powerful muscles rippling with iridescent light. You feel the dingo's awesomeness. Finally, the dingo curls up and lays down.

Very deliberately, the dingo turns its head and looks you squarely in the eyes. Its eyes are a brilliant, deep red. Your upper body presses backward with the intensity of its eyes.

At this time, I, Lynn, place crystals at the four corners of the circle of sand painting. I had been waiting for the moment of power, the confrontation of the eyes. Your eyes of light meeting the eyes of darkness. Now four huge and shining crystals illuminate the four corners of our circle.

The smoke from the fire gets mixed into the illumination of the east crystal, the crystal of vision, of creativity, of clear sight. Remember that we are bringing the darkness into focus in order to more clearly define the light.

The dingo is still vibrating with fierce energy. Suddenly, there is a corridor of illumination from the east crystal rising up through the smoke of the fire. With quiet, controlled steps the dingo rises, then begins walking up the lit corridor toward the sky and looking back at us from time to time to be sure we are following. We do follow. Our bodies are made of spirit, and we are walking up this lighted corridor, though it feels as if each of our bodies is under a tremendous pressure. It feels like walking on the bottom of the ocean under tons of water. Feel your body protected by the cocoonlike cloud still around you like a protective womb. We are being forced up through the crust of consciousness. Allow me to hold your hand. We are all together in the struggle for consciousness.

As we hold hands, you begin to see the skin somehow melting off my bones. At first you feel shock and revulsion, but this quickly passes. You now know the same thing is happening to you. You see the blue-white bones of my skeleton still holding your hands. You look down and witness your own skeleton.

Breathe evenly and slowly, concentrate, and do not be afraid. Trust your warrior spirit, and keep on moving toward the light that you now see at the end of the cloud tunnel. We keep walking together. As you focus on the light, become aware that it is actually emanating from the entrance to a cave.

Notice that the dingo has run ahead of us and disappeared over a lip of a bluishly iridescent rock.

We enter the cave and see Oruncha of Chauritzi standing tall and powerful in the center of the cave. Oruncha is a God of the Skyworld. He initiates. He is wearing his clever bag full of magic crystals. His eyes are piercing. They miss nothing. His attitude is one of welcome. Do not judge or fear what is occurring. Look out through your skull at the ethereal magnificence of your surroundings. Pieces of rainbow light are shimmering in the cave walls as if chips of the sun and the moon or the stars are embedded there.

Now hear Oruncha speak. He says,

Crystal Beings, take your strength from the stars in the galaxies. You are as if at the bottom of the sea; you have reached Krakkam's domain. You are *muru*, blessed with life. Pick, each, a pearl shell and a *roré*, a sacred crystal, from the walls of the cave. Long ago the women held the sacred *rangas* for the people. That tradition was lost and given to the male clans, and slowly we lost our way in terror and imbalance. But the people will rise again with a new balance. The power of Mother Nature cannot be ignored or forgotten. We honor your presence here. Be not afraid of hearing the bull roarer or taking part in the rites of men or women. What belongs truly to men will forever be theirs, and what is of woman will always be theirs. There is a balance in wisdom and all change is a miracle to behold. You are made from the elements, and to the elements you must one day return. You are now given a chance to view with honor your own skeleton, the true structure that holds your physical body together, the skeleton that has so often been associated with fear. Do not be afraid. All is well. Your Spirit lives in your bones.

Now, go over to the dry stone walls of the cave, walls that feel like hardened sap from a tree, and finally pick out a glistening pearl shell and a crystal that throws prisms of purple light all around you. These just fit into the palm of your bony hand. Walking seems difficult now, as if your skeleton is weighted down by an unseen force.

Notice now in your mind's eye that Oruncha is seated on the cave floor. A small fire burns, and the dingo sits off at a respectful distance, his shiny paws at the edge of a circle that you and I are now joining. We sit with great effort and place the crystals on a mat in front of us. The mat holds the designs of the constellations carved into its bark.

Oruncha says,

Hold the pearl shells, Crystal People, as we journey together. The *karari*, or pearl shells, are sacred to me. Years ago they were worn over our pubic hair. By your being here, you are bringing back balance to yourself and to all people. When we begin to heal ourselves, we make a change in all people, just like a tiny pebble makes ripples on the lake. You have much yet to learn, but you have ventured into the mysteries of Oruncha with trust and innocence. You are rewarded for your trials with the eyes of Oruncha. The *rore*, the sacred crystals, are my eyes. Use them as your own. Look into the crystal now and ask any darkness in your life to reveal itself.

In the silence, allow the image, sense, feelings of any darkness to appear in your crystal. Notice what you see, feel, hear, who or what appears; notice everything.

Trust that whatever appears is an area of darkness, a symbol or relationship or a situation to be healed, to work on. Maybe someone you dislike intensely appears. He or she represents some quality to be healed in you.

Dialogue with whom or whatever appears. Allow your mind to trust, and dialogue even if what appears is a symbol or object. Let the object speak. Take some silent time to do this.

Now allow this person, symbol, or object of darkness to reveal to you in what area of your life you must focus: on being more aware of your darkness, your negative side, your naivete, or your fear? What do you need to let go of?

Accept a gift from the image of darkness. This gift is a piece of black obsidian. Take it in thanks and remembrance of this journey so that in spirit you will always remember the gift that darkness brings.

Darkness allows us to truly live in the light. By honoring and knowing our own darkness, we can fully live in the light. Take a moment to examine the obsidian.

Now Oruncha speaks,

> Take blessings and take heart. You have journeyed well. Take with you the crystal, the pearl shell, and the piece of obsidian. Somehow, in waking life, have these objects close to your heart, either in your spirit sight always or carry the actual objects in your medicine or clever bag. I give thanks for your journey and efforts from all the beings of the Dreamtime.

As Oruncha finishes speaking, you and I move almost as fast as fire dances, move back down the lit corridor of smoke in our skeletons. As we move down the corridor, we become aware that our flesh is returning to our bodies, that we had to be stripped clean only to enter the sacred cave, and now our bodies are fully our own again as we reach the ground where the sand painting is.

Notice now that you have, in the sacred Dreamtime, the crystal, pearl shell, and piece of black obsidian in the palm of your fleshy hand. Place them, as you like, on your sand painting.

Rest easy. Breathe naturally. Begin to sense your body in all its wondrousness. Begin to move your limbs slightly. As you focus on your breathing, become aware of being in a room, being fully in your body. Whenever you are ready, open your eyes and come back fully into your body and into the room.

I would like you to get some obsidian, a crystal, and a pearl shell and put them in a very special bag. Remember Oruncha of Chauritzi.

WORKSHEET

What darkness within yourself did you become aware of? How did you feel about the dingo? Did he inspire fear or trust? Did you find it difficult to trust yourself as you moved more deeply into the Dreamtime? How did you feel? Describe that briefly.

Describe your sand painting. Describe the colors and the design. Draw it as well as you can.

Describe your sacred Dreamtime wilderness place. Briefly describe the ten large stones that you gathered. How did you feel when you placed the red ochre earth on your body? Describe its texture. How did you feel about your body once it was covered in red ochre?

Write down your prayer of thanks. Write down your power song again so that it becomes more deeply imprinted in your mind.

How did Oruncha of Chauritzi affect you? What did he say of particular interest to you? What area of your being must you focus on and be aware of, that holds darkness or negativity for you, naivete or fear? What do you need to let go of? Describe.

Describe what the crystal, the pearl shell, and the piece of black obsidian meant to you. What relationship in your life needs to be healed?

Chapter 9

Goowawas

Introduction

The Goowawas are like fairies or wood spirits. They are the little people of the aboriginal world of Australia. This is another meditation to help exercise your trust, particularly in the Dreamtime. Trust what you imagine because, again, remember that what you imagine is real. The Goowawas are forgotten people. They want to be known to you, to be your allies, to help you. This meditation is to heal your heart.

Exercise/Meditation

We will journey to a wilderness place. The trees are lush, and you can hear many birds in the distance. Notice that you feel calm, alert, and joyous. We are beginning a good journey, a heart journey. Take a few moments in silence to feel yourself settling into this wild and wondrous place.

It is evening, when the world changes. The moon is becoming visible high in the sky. Tonight we will work with the crystals and the Goowawas, the little people.

Goowawas are like fairies, wood spirits. They live in a cave near here. They help with dreaming in the Sacred Dreamtime. Tonight we will leave food for them. They are always hungry. The Goowawas are very good, but you have to be careful of them. They're extremely emotional and can have bad tempers. You don't want to make them mad. You must never lie to them, and you must always keep your word.

Imagine, feel, place your consciousness in the middle of your body, two inches below your belly button, the place of power, the place of *Ki*, or one-point, as martial artists might say, the place of will. Hold your power here and breathe deeply. This is a time for pulling back the bow. Take a few minutes in silence to center you energy here. Know that you are safe and protected and no harm can come to you on your journey.

Now imagine yourself in a clearing in the forest. You can smell the great eucalyptus trees nearby. See near you a sand painting made out of colored sand on the ground. See the painting made up of spirals with a center spiral as its focus. The spiral circles to the right.

See many crystals on the sand painting, and notice how you feel when the crystals shine from the light of the moon and the fire nearby. Feel the warmth inside your body.

Know now that Goowawas are waist high. They are forgotten people, proud spirits, wonderful in their magical ways, and know many things.

Walk around the painting clockwise and then sit down. As you are sitting now in front of the sand painting, realize that one of the crystals is calling for you. She will ask for you and show you her colors. Take a few minutes in silence to allow the crystal to call you and to feel her presence inside you. Dream with this crystal and follow her with your eyes. Note what color and configuration this crystal is.

The crystal you are seeing has great beauty. The crystal is made up of physical things and it is part of this earthly world. But she has something more than beauty, just like the mountains do. We say in the Dreamtime that the Great Spirit is forever and we are forever. You might say that if I took a chip off that crystal, it would be less, but it would still be part of the Dreamtime. You might say that if I take something out of the crystal, she will be reduced, but I say that the crystal is part of the whole; therefore, it can never be reduced. Its beauty is the key. The crystal is more than the sum of her minerals and atoms. Like the mountains, she has beauty. Beauty is the essence. Beauty is part of the higher arithmetic of the Dreamtime. Certain things add—one, two, three—regularlike. When you enter the Dreamtime, your concept of arithmetic must change. There is beauty in this sand painting, and there is also the sacredness of life.

Watch now as the colors in the sand painting, your colors, begin to move. The colors will sparkle; then wavy lines may begin to undulate back and forth.

The name of this sand painting is Goowawa Dreaming. The Goowawas are a forgotten race. Inside each of us is a forgotten person. That forgotten person is represented also by the dots on the sand painting, which also represent the Goowawas. Because whatever is outside is inside, as above, so below. Each of these dots represents self unrealized. The painting helps us realize and bring together what has never before had life. For this ceremony to work and have power, there must be intuition and insight, self-realization. The Goowawas like us to search deeply inside ourselves. That's more food for the little people, so they can be remembered. Notice that there is a dark edge around the painting. It represents the abominable darkness. We fall into that darkness when we fail to see the inward wholeness, when we fail to balance our inward intuition with our outward actions. See, the moon is high now. Let's ask the Goowawas to join our ceremony.

Breath deeply and relax even more deeply. Be aware of a force of high energy around and inside you. This energy is powerful and moves your head back as you look deeper into the Dreamtime. See in the dirt before you baby tracks of the little people. Notice that you sense a presence; something else has entered with a new rush of energy. The Goowawas have joined us to help us rediscover what has been lost in ourselves. Take a few minutes in silence to give thanks to the Goowawas and trust, trust yourself in this new way of the Dreamtime. Shake the hands of the Goowawas. Look in their eyes and honor them.

Each of us forgets what is important in life. We forget until something jolts us and forces us to remember—an illness, a death, a major change in job, a relationship. We must learn to remember, and the crystals and the Goowawas help us do this.

Now take in your spirit hands the crystal that called you earlier. Feel how the weight of it seems almost to grow as you now hold it in your hands. Pray silently as you physically merge with your crystal. Then see the crystal become mirrorlike. See your own face and the Goowawas sitting around you. They are sitting on their heels in a meditative state, helping you. Let the crystal rest on your solar plexus.

Now mentally take out pictures of people who are in your heart. Take some time here to remember them, to heal and begin to soothe old wounds, or to find new insights about your own paths of heart. Know and tell yourself that you'll consciously remember whatever is important to remember about this heart talk afterwards. Watch the Goowawas talking to you. They are telling you that to move on into the New Age successfully, you must demand that old emotional pains be dealt with and released.

Let us begin by calling up the image of your father. Even if you never met your father, let an image appear. Know that every person who comes now comes to bring you a gift. The gift may be tangible, a song, stone, or flower, but also a gift of insight and wisdom, from the highest part of themselves.

Now hug your father and dialogue with him. I'll give you a few moments. Take a deep breath of spirit. Whatever pain or negativity you feel, blow it into the crystal.

Let that image fade away.

Bring up the image of your mother. Now dialogue with your mother. Notice her beauty in the Dreamtime. And remember that sadness, anger, even fear can be gifts to work with, to lead us into transformation. Blow any discomfort into the crystal.

Let the image fade away.

Bring up the images of any brothers and dialogue with them. If you had no brothers, dialogue with someone in your life who was or is like a brother. Take a few moments to do this. Blow negativity into your crystal.

Let that image fade away.

Now bring up the images of sisters and dialogue with them. Dialogue with anyone who was like a sister if you had no sisters. What is the gift she brings? Take time in the silence to explore. Blow negativity into your crystal.

Let the image fade away.

Bring up a lover or a past lover if none is present in your life now. Dialogue with that person, and consider what he or she says and how you feel about it. Keep the crystal on your hands and know that the crystal is helping you to heal, helping you toward self-realization. Any problem you have with this person, solve it. Blow negativity into your crystal.

Let the image fade away.

Now ask yourself who is the most important person to talk with. Bring him or her up and dialogue with this person. Why has this person come? What messages and gifts does he or she bring? How do you feel about this person coming? Blow negativity into your crystal.

Let the image fade away.

Take a deep breath, and bring up the image of one of your grandfathers. If you never met him, call up an image of him anyway. He is one of the forgotten people. Remember him and share. Blow any negativity into your crystal.

Let the image fade.

Now call up your other grandfather. Blow any negativity into your crystal.

And now one of your grandmothers. Blow any negativity into your crystal.

Now your other grandmother. Blow any negativity into your crystal.

Now ask yourself whom else you need to dialogue with.

Remember now that feelings are the way to achieve freedom. Feelings are a path to freedom. Let your feelings be free and pay attention. If no conversation comes, let your feelings be your guide. Feel into the person who comes to be with you. Each of us has forgotten people in our lives whom we need to access and crystallize our feelings toward. Let yourself be guided by your feelings. Take time in the silence to relax and release and remember. Blow negativity into your crystal.

Now ask yourself once more whom you need to contact. Trust whoever comes to be an important person for some reason. Even if you do not know why you have called up this person from within the depths of your imagination, the crystal power of your being has called this person up for a reason. Dialogue and find out what there is to learn. Take some time to do this.

Now we are near the end of our journey. Begin to notice this wilderness place you are in. Remember this place, for it is a place you can return to at any time. The gift of this place is the gift of remembrance, the gift of uncovering what has been lost or hidden. Hold hands with the Goowawas and with them give thanks for this place. Mark it in your memory so it can be a place of power for you.

Now that you have fixed this place in imagination and memory, stand up with your crystal and begin to walk to another place. Find a soft spot out of view of your power place. You may walk half a mile before you come to a proper place. The Goowawas come with you and help you.

Sit down in the soft dirt and begin to dig a hole. The Goowawas help you move the dirt. You are digging a hole to bury your crystal. The power that the crystal has helped you elicit is now inside you, vibrating in your feelings, in your heart. The crystal has absorbed any pain, sadness, or hurt from all your dialogues, and now is the time to give your sadnesses back to the earth. The earth is our mother, and she can heal all. Release all the people you have called up from any blame and responsibility for your life, right now. Take some silent time to do this.

Hold the crystal up to the Great Spirit with your left hand. Now bury the crystal, and begin to notice as you do that your heart *chakra*, this whole area of your body, begins to feel warm, as if a crystal has been placed in your heart *chakra*. This is so, for all of us have a crystal in our hearts, and only the blocks of our relationships, the blocks of our past, keep us from achieving the healing of our heart wounds.

The Goowawas are standing in a circle around you. They are pleased. Take time in the silence to be aware of your body. Be aware of the feeling in your heart as one of the Goowawas smiles at you and places her tiny hand on your heart (chest). Look into her eyes. The Goowawa helps you finish burying the crystal as you smooth the dirt and release the bonds of the past. You feel lighter. You feel a subtle lessening of tension in you chest. Remember this feeling.

The Goowawas now hold both your hands. Tell yourself once again that you will remember everything that is necessary to remember, of the new feeling in your heart, of the many dialogues you have had. Give thanks to the Goowawas and yourself for the work you are doing. Take a moment as you give thanks. Once again remember the wilderness place of the sand painting, the place of the forgotten people, the Goowawas. Tell yourself silently that you will always remember them and know that this place is a tangible tool, a place loaded with power and gifts for you to use for the rest of your life. All you must do is desire and choose to go there and see them. When next you journey there, remember the feeling of light that lives in your chest. This is your inner heart crystal. Keep your energy centered on this inner heart crystal when you do dialogues in the future. This heart crystal will be a good guide to self-healing.

And remember also that our Mother Earth and the Goowawas will take and disperse all sadnesses.

Now begin to release the vision of your wilderness place and focus your attention on your breathing. Let breath be your guide back from the sacred Dreamtime as you become aware, fully aware, of your body, giving yourself permission to move your limbs gently. At your own pace, return fully to your body, come back fully into the room, and open your eyes.

WORKSHEET

Describe your sand painting, the crystals in it, and their placement. Who are the people that you found in your heart? What were the wounds that you needed to heal? What new insights did you find about your own path of heart? Describe.

Describe the Goowawas you saw and how they felt to you. What did they say to you? Describe how you felt about your mother. How did it feel to see members of your family, your sisters, and your brothers in the Dreamtime? Who was the lover who came to mind? Describe the dialogue that you had with him or her.

Who is the forgotten person in your life? A grandparent? Describe that person and how you felt about him or her. Who else did you need to dialogue with? Describe that dialogue and the feelings that you had.

What did the wilderness place that you found look like, and how did it affect you? What effect will this meditation with the Goowawas have on your life? Describe the sadnesses you dispensed with.

My ancestors, my allies, my medicine, and all those who love me, thank you for joining me on my shaman path. For you, Great Wind, who takes my messages to the Great Spirit, I give thanks. Ho!

—Ginevee

Chapter 10

Oruncha of Chauritzi

Introduction

This visualization process and meditation have to do with strengthening your trust, exercising your ability to give up your physical being as you know it to the Great Spirit or to a messenger from the Great Spirit who happens to be in this meditation, the Sky Being, Oruncha of Chauritzi.

Oruncha is a Sky Being, an ancestor figure I met in my work in Australia with Ginevee, the aboriginal woman who is a member of the Sisterhood of the Shields. The way I worked with Oruncha is not at all the way he works with aborigini apprentices. He worked with me as a white woman, and he worked with me in a way that was an effort to bridge one culture with another, one understanding of shamanism with a different understanding of the power of woman.

His process with me was always a tearing down of old structural habits and a building and implanting of the new. He will be implanting in you crystals of knowledge and of wisdom. They act as windows to higher consciousness, windows into your private and personal *akashic* record. In other words, the crystals act as gateways leading into your most private and powerful source of power, the all knowing, the all knowable sea of intelligence that is part of the Great Spirit, that is so often so very difficult to access.

This visualization is not designed to be frightening or gruesome in any way. Tearing the body apart and replacing it with a more intelligent design is a normal aspect of shamanism and an aspect I have found throughout the world when I have worked with the Sisterhood of the Shields almost anywhere. One way or another, the shaman initiation has to do with tearing apart the old and rebuilding the physical and therefore the spiritual body into something new and more effective for spiritual work.

As with all these meditations, a worksheet is provided at the end.

As you come out of this deep trance that I hope you will reach in your work with Oruncha, be sure to write down all your impressions and feelings so you have them in your notebook.

Exercise/Meditation

Now we will begin a journey. In your mind's eye, in your imagination, see or feel or visualize or imagine yourself in a wilderness place. You are journeying to a place of power, a place that lives inside you, a wild place.

As you imagine yourself in this wild place, see yourself with bare feet. Your feet touch soft ground, fine dirt, earth. Feel the warmth of the earth, and realize how our Mother Earth protects us and is protecting you now. As you do this, sing your power song to yourself. Take a moment to do this.

Knowing you are protected and safe, begin to look around you. See a large boulderlike stone nearby. See many tall trees. Notice that you are in an amphitheater setting. There is a grassy area nearby.

As you begin to feel comfortable here, notice the bright colors, the flowers, the look of the trees, the alert and poised way you feel in this place. Take a few minutes to feel, sense, touch, and smell, in your imagination, this wild place.

Now go over and place your hands on the large boulder. This is a stone called power rock. Feel the smooth surface. Be aware that it feels as if many hands have touched this surface; the stone feels slick and smooth, wonderful; also notice that you feel as if you are the first and only one ever to touch this power rock. Both knowings are true. Many have touched this power rock and been given new strength, and you are the very first person to touch this stone because your power is a primal power, a link back to creation itself. As you place your hands in the ancient hollows of the rock, you realize that the worn indentations exactly fit your hands. Once they are placed, you realize that, for a moment, you cannot lift your hands away. A pleasant shock wave goes up your arms and through your body. You feel electrified by the ancient power of the rock. This is an initiation rock that has been used for centuries to clear away energy blocks in the bodies of apprentices. You might feel a distinct tingling sensation. Look at the tiny pieces of mica in the rock, and note how you see their reflection with more intense clarity.

Be aware that with each breath you are feeling more relaxed, comfortable, and joyous. Now take you hands away from the rock.

After receiving the new surge of energy from power rock, in your mind's eye, see yourself taking off your clothes because we all must go naked into the Dreamtime. As you take off your clothes, our normal societal protection, be aware that here, now, in the Sacred Dreamtime, you actually feel more protected in your naked openness. Realize that you are in the Sacred Dreamtime and that your body has the form of the physical, but is really in spirit.

After you remove your clothes, you are drawn to move to another place nearby, around the corner of the stone. You are drawn to an area of shadow beneath a grove of eucalyptus trees. As you walk toward the trees, a female figure emerges from the darkness. It is an old American Indian woman who wears her hair in long grey braids. She wears a long, blue skirt and a blouse with shiny red and yellow ribbons hanging in streamers from her shoulders. There are red beaded moccasins on her feet. You recognize her as Agnes Whistling Elk. She is carrying something for you in her arms. She holds a folded bundle out to you. Agnes smiles at you with a twinkle of light in her eyes. You are delighted to see her, but there is a question in your eyes. As if reading your mind she speaks to you:

> Sometimes woman must be initiated by man, just as man must sometimes be initiated by woman. I am here as your guardian; it is because of me that you are here. It is time we met. This is for you and has been worn by your sisters and brothers before you. There are no cultural boundaries in the Dreamtime.

You look into Agnes's brilliantly clear eyes as you take the bundle. You slowly begin to unwrap it. In it you find a kangaroo robe to place around you. The robe feels warm and sensuous as you put it on. You give thanks for the animal that has given away to you in order for you to wear this healing robe. "Know that this robe is the robe of the Seven Sister Stars of the Pleiades," Agnes tells you.

Now in your mind's eye visualize that it is getting to be twilight, the time when the earth changes, the time of true power and mystery. Yet know and feel that you are safe, protected by your higher spirit, by the kangaroo robe, by the powers in all the four directions in the Sacred Dreamtime, and by Agnes, who walks behind you and to your left.

You look up and notice striations of clouds blowing over the moon that is becoming visible. Welcoming the night, you give thanks for the silence. You know that you are waiting and working for healing and power. Take a few minutes in silence to honor the change from light to dark in the Sacred Dreamtime and to again give thanks for the way you are honoring and loving yourself by giving yourself this gift of a journey. You sense the nearness of Agnes, but her presence does not distract you.

Now see yourself beginning to build a small fire. Agnes and you gather wood. The fire feels warm and nurturing. Notice how fire can feel like a true friend.

Agnes sits across the fire from you in meditation. You sing your power song to yourself. You begin to hear scraping sounds, whooshing sounds. You turn, and projected on the power rock behind you, from out of the reflections of your fire, you see a shadow on the wall of rock. Then the shadow takes the form of giant wings. Be aware that you do not feel fear. You glance at Agnes, but her eyes are closed. A welcoming spirit inside you tells you that all is well. As you stare at the now moving shadow, you begin to see the head of a tall crow, the size of an ostrich. As the crow appears in the firelight, your eyes and the crow's eyes hold each other in a long gaze. You are fascinated by this magnificent creature.

Soon the figure of the crow recedes and from behind the power rock comes an awesome looking man. He is a tall, bearded aborigine warrior with a red band around his head. He is covered with surreal white and red-ochre designs. With powerful strides, he dances wildly around you; then he motions for you to follow him down a trail around behind the power rock. You walk, trustingly, next to him, for what seems like a very long time. Agnes follows at a distance.

As you walk, the sky begins to change. You realize you cannot tell whether you have been walking all night or have just gone to another place in the Dreamtime where it is lighter. You realize that time does not matter in this spirit world, and you let the thought go. Suddenly the warrior turns and in one fast and powerful movement throws a jute bag over your entire body. He ties it at your feet and effortlessly throws you over his shoulder like a bag of corn. At first you're horrified and frightened because you cannot see anything. The bag is strongly woven, so tightly it could carry water. You become aware of this warrior's sure, even stride. He carries you up and down hills for a long time. Then suddenly he drops you gently to the ground and removes the sack. You look around for Agnes and see her sitting nearby. She nods her head to you.

You are now sitting by a river in a grassy meadow. You listen to the sounds of water and to bellbirds chirping in the treees, their voices like tiny, clear chimes.

You instinctively lie down to rest. You feel a little strange, as if you have moved into a new and unfamiliar dimension. You notice the shadow of the crow nearby, and you feel very comfortable. Then the warrior comes up next to you. He is holding what can only be described as a power stick. The stick is about a foot long, wrapped in leather, with a very clear crystal attached to one end. The crystal is long and is covered at the end attached to the stick with red cloth. You study the dark face of this man. He appears to have the wisdom of someone very ancient, but his face is not old. His eyes, like polished mirrors, are too powerful for you to look into for long. Suddenly, he leaps into the air and shrieks. Then he dances around you for several minutes holding the power stick above his head.

Then the warrior stands poised above you, takes the stick, and moves it over your body. He pushes you gently to lie down. The ground feels warm from the sun as you lie next to the slowly moving river. Agnes sits behind you and cradles your head in her lap. Her eyes are closed, and she is in deep meditation. You can tell that the warrior is performing something akin to psychic surgery because you feel as if you are being gently split open down the middle. You are surprised at how normal and protected you feel even with this unusual ceremony. You realize that no harm could ever come to you here in the Sacred Dreamtime. Here your body has the form of the physical but is really in spirit. You know Agnes will protect you.

Then the warrior speaks. His voice is deep and heavily accented. He says,

> My name is Oruncha of Chauritzi. I am a medicine spirit
> warrior. I am Crazy One, the Hermaphrodite. I have killed

you so that you may live. This bird is Crow. He is your nari, your medicine familiar. He is a clever bird, and he will guard you always. You must die to your old ways to enter the Sacred Dreamtime. I have drawn a spiral circle design next to you on the ground. Give me your finger.

With these words, Oruncha holds his huge hands over your body. Then he takes your fingers, and together you trace the spiral design on the ground next to you. You feel the grit of the sand.

Take a few minutes to experience the design.

"This spiral is your childhood. Imagine and see designs that would symbolize your childhood," Oruncha says, tracing what looks like the innermost circle. "Here in this spiral is represented the growth and experiences you have had in your life." As your fingers trace the spiral design, be aware that you feel that the spiral connects somehow to the middle of your body, to the center of your being. Feel the pull in your solar plexus.

Now, with your body opened by the power of Oruncha, Oruncha begins to chant and sing a song. You cannot understand the words, but they settle you like your own power song. Crow helps by flapping his wings over your body in a drumming, blessing way.

Oruncha next takes many crystals out of his clever bag, his medicine bag. The bag is made of fiber. It is red and blue striped, about two feet long and one foot wide. Here Oruncha keeps his sacred objects. He says,

> I am going to add light and wisdom to your inner body. I am going to place crystals inside your spirit body so that you will always be strengthened and protected. These will be placed in strategic places, and you can call on this energy whenever you need strength, insight, intuition in any aspect of your life.

Oruncha now holds up the first crystal in silent prayer to the sun. He places this first crystal in your heart area. Immediately, you feel warmer, as if your temperature suddenly has risen. Oruncha says, "This heart crystal will give you greater openness and ability to express love."

Oruncha proceeds throughout the trunk of your body. You look down and witness the whole operation. It's as if you've had a spinal block. You see your whole midsection and chest laid open without any blood or pain. Occasionally, Agnes strokes your hair. As he works with you, Oruncha says,

> This crystal is small yet powerful. I place it near your throat, the beginning of your high spiritual *chakras*, where you will have even greater expression of high spiritual truths and a freedom to express your emotions.
> This larger crystal is for your lungs. This for a sense of personal power and freedom. Take a few minutes in silence to feel the new breath moving into and out of your lungs.
> Now look into your stomach. Here, this perfect Herkamer crystal will help you to digest all of life. Know that all life is in proper order. Take this silent time to begin digestion with the help of this healing crystal.
> No, see your liver. Your liver is located on your right side below your lungs. The liver represents your will to live. This shooting or directing crystal will help you keep on a strong path with great will. In the silence, see the force of this double terminated crystal entering and doing its work within you.
> Now look at your pancreas. I am placing a crystal here. Your pancreas is located on your left side under the lungs. The pancreas represents female courage, doing those things we associate with the feminine, such as fearless intuition, courage to follow your dreams, and receptivity.
> Your gall bladder is located on your right side near your liver. It represents male courage, such as being successful in the world and strength to stand up for your convictions. This amethyst crystal will aid you. You can focus on this crystal when you need help in the area of male courage.

After Oruncha has completed his medicine work of helping and healing your body with sacred crystals, he again takes his power stick and, folding the layers of your skin and muscle together, he completely closes up your spirit body. Again, you feel no pain, everything feels normal, and you are pleased with the awareness and relaxation you are experiencing.

Oruncha places his two warm hands lightly all over your body. The crow is again flapping his wings in unison to the prayer Oruncha is singing quietly,

> You are well. You are better than you have ever been. The great things of the earth, the stones, the light of the crystals are inside you. There is peace and awareness throughout your body. The darkness will never again be so black for you, because I have given you tools to use, energy to draw on, the power to heal yourself, to tune yourself to the vibrations of this loving earth. Let yourself accept and use this strength. Accept and use this gift. Let yourself say silently: I accept. I accept. I accept my new self. I accept myself. I accept this gift of myself.

Now the crow stops flapping his wings, and Oruncha holds his hands over your belly. Here is where many of our fears and anxieties get lodged. You can feel heat emanating from Oruncha's hands, and he says,

> I am drawing the sacred spiral design that is also drawn next to you in the earth, the same design that earlier you traced with your fingers. Now with my healing hands, I am drawing this design on your belly. Whenever you need more energy, whenever you need to center yourself or free up emotions, not only can you call on the crystals within you, but you can retrace this design. Whenever you retrace this design, you will recall the dream that is you. Trace this design in a clockwise movement with the flat of your hand.

Take a few minutes in silence to feel and picture the spiral design being drawn on your belly. Know that you now have many tools within you to help you on the path of enlightenment.

Now look Oruncha of Chauritzi in the eyes. Once more let your eyes hold each other's gaze. See his dark skin, his beard, and the red band around his forehead. Silently give thanks for his presence. Know that what you are feeling is a genuine trust and love. Give thanks as you embrace each other and then as you watch him and the crow leave.

With Agnes holding your hand, you revel in the silence of your wilderness place. Know peace is within you. Now place your consciousness once again on your physical body, letting go of the Dreamtime and Agnes's hand. You see her back away and disappear. Focus attention on your breath. Breathe easily. In your own time, begin to move your body, sense your limbs becoming fully present in your body, and when you are ready, open your eyes and return with new gifts.

WORKSHEET

Describe power rock and how it felt under your hands. Describe how it felt to be naked in the Dreamtime.

Describe how Agnes Whistling Elk appeared to you, what she was
wearing, and how it made you feel to have a conversation with her, to
be near her. When Agnes handed you the robe of the Seven Sister Stars
of the Pleiades, how did it make you feel?

Describe Oruncha of Chauritzi and how he made you feel. Where did
Oruncha place the crystals inside your body? Describe how you sensed
them within you. Did they add light and wisdom to your inner body?
How do you feel that this work with the crystals will affect your everyday life? Is it difficult for you to accept this gift? Discuss this.

Draw the spiral design that Oruncha drew on your belly. Meditate on that design and sense how it concerns the meaning of all life.

Chapter 11

Weapons of the Warrior and Medicine Woman in Crystal

Introduction

Every warrior and warrioress needs weapons with which to move out into the world, into the physical world or the spiritual world. Each weapon has a meaning. A shield, for instance, is not only a shield for protection; its designs also tell the world about your spiritual path. A spear has the ability to hit its mark. In other words, you are not only standing poised in your life ready to attack the problems that you know exist, but you are ready to fight for your own ability to survive and to become your destiny. In your emotional life, the axe can chop away at old conditionings, feelings, and emotions that you are through with, that you no longer need to carry. The axe can be both your defense and an instrument for your aggression.

Choose your weapons carefully as you proceed into this meditation. We often carry a bow and arrow within us, and we spend our entire lives pulling back the bow and never shooting the arrow because we never define the target, the target, perhaps, being our act of power.

The drum gives you the ability to imitate the heartbeat of Mother Earth. The drum allows you to sing, to send messages, to dance your joy, to sing your song. There are symbols of thunder and lightning on the drum. The drum can call the powers of the higher beings to mediate with the powers of Mother Earth.

The obsidian blade has a handle made of elk horn. The obsidian blade is a magnificent mirror of magic. It also can cut the luminous fibers that bind you to situations that you no longer need or should be involved with. When I took the marriage basket back to the dreamers, to the Sisterhood, I had to cut away the fibers of an evil sorcerer with the obsidian blade. It is a great weapon and gives you great strength.

A personal pipe is important for prayer. It is important to learn how to pray, to give something away to the Great Spirit, which gave you life. It is important to learn to go within and find your gratitude and your humbleness and your desires for making your life more complete.

This meditation is about choosing your weapons in life and finding your medicine woman within.

For this meditation, you also need a small crystal that you can carry with you on your person, a crystal that you will never use for anything else, ever. It is going to be the home of your medicine woman, the medicine woman that will be your wise one within, your guide on your path so that when you are without your teacher, when you are somewhere alone in the world and you need counseling, you will have this being with you. After this meditation, you will know how to make contact with her, and you will preserve her power within the crystal. Always wrap this crystal in red, natural material and keep it in one of your power bundles, or you could wear it inside a pouch. So think of those things when you pick out the crystal. If you are going to wear it in a medicine pouch around your neck, obviously you want it to be a smaller crystal. Be sure that the crystal is quartz and speaks to you in a very, very special way. Also, it should be a beautiful crystal to provide an environment that your medicine woman would be pleased with, remembering that beauty is part of her spirit. She would be incapable of doing anything ugly in the spirit world or in this world.

In a sense, the medicine woman within you is an enhancer or a translator. She helps you to access the knowledge that is held in your subconscious mind. If you cannot make what is in your subconscious mind conscious, then there is no way to access that knowledge except through dreams and visions. Therefore, we have many beings and forces of energy within the shamanistic tradition that help us access that wisdom and make it part of our daily lives. That is one of the main reasons I want you to know this medicine woman living within yourself and make contact with her. She has always been with you, from the day you were born. It's just that you have not understood that this energy force is within you. During this visualization, it will become very obvious to you that she has always been there and has been waiting a long time to meet you, to communicate with you. It's also important to remember to ask her when will be a good time to see her on a daily or weekly basis. These beings need your light and your energy to become more visible to you. The more time you spend with them, the more strongly they are able to communicate messages and meanings and answers to your questions.

Exercise/Meditation

Pick out a very special crystal, one you love and will use for nothing else. You will use this crystal to call your medicine woman.

Lie down and place your crystal on your chest in a position that is comfortable, so you can forget about it for a while. Take a deep breath and feel the crystal harmonizing with the beat of your heart.

You will take a journey. You will begin by finding in your mind's eye, in your imagination, a new wilderness place, a place you have never been to before in any of your journeys. In finding this wilderness place, you feel like you have found your home, a place that will unfold itself inside your imagination like a shining crystal itself. This may be a desert place of wide open vistas, red mountains, low creosote bushes, clean dirt, and bright sun. You may journey to the ocean, to a clear blue ocean shore, where the shore birds sing with crisp voices, where the wind is full in your hair, where the beauty of the waves reminds you of your own inner beauty and power. You may travel to the forest, where the rich smell of the trees fills your lungs, where the green color brightens your spirit, where you feel safe yet free in the wilderness before you. Or you may travel in your imagination to a high mountain place, a place of steep cliffs that command respect, a place where a high mountain lake, blue and green, has risen below the snow-topped peaks. Even here you can still feel the warm sun pour down on you. Go. We will all find our own wilderness place, a new place, a place of joy and discovery, a place of freedom and also disciplined action, a place of growth, a place of gathering love, nourishment, strength.

Take a few minutes in silence to discover your special wilderness place.

As you begin to see yourself in your wilderness place, once again notice the sounds you imagine are there. The wind. Birds. Any animals that may be in the area. Now pay attention to any smells. Can you smell the ocean, some small plants in the area? Does your own skin smell different in this wilderness place? Take a few minutes in silence to begin to walk around and become familiar with your wilderness place. Touch the ground, the sand, or the dirt. Feel the bark of trees. Let yourself be guided by your desires. Let yourself come to know this place like a new home.

Now I would like everyone to find a power spot, a place that feels just right. Find a place large enough to build a sacred wheel.

When you've found your power spot, I want you to look down at your spirit body in the Dreamtime and notice that you are carrying a pouch around your waist. Standing at your power spot, open your pouch and find tobacco and four beautiful crystals there. These crystals have been given to you as a gift by the powers of the Dreamtime. Make a sacred wheel, walking clockwise and spreading pinches of tobacco. Now walk around the sacred wheel to the four directions and place a crystal in each of the directions. As you begin to do this, make a short prayer in each direction.

Standing at the center of your sacred wheel, begin in the east. Powers of the east, place of the sunrise, place of creativity and illumination, place of birth, place of the *heyoka* or trickster, place of the eagle who flies highest and sees farthest, place of the hawk, who like older brother eagle is a messenger to the spirit world, place of the coyote always around at the creation of earth, always ready to bring humor to serious situations. Powers of the east, whose color is yellow like the sun, come in to guide and be with us now. Now you add, in silence, a personal prayer to the east as you place your east crystal down in your sacred wheel.

Now turn to the south. Powers of the south, place of innocence and trust, place of taking things one step at a time, place of seeing what is directly before you, home of the childlike wonder in all of us, place of the sacred mouse, who sees what is in front of its face, place of the gathering squirrel who takes one step at a time and plans for hard winters, place of water, flowing over rocks, place of the dolphin in the sea, trusting and wise. The color of green or red, sacred place of change, of discovery, powers of the south come in to guide and be with us now. And now, in silence, add a personal prayer to the south as you place your south crystal down in its proper place on your sacred wheel.

Turning to the west, say powers of the west, home of intuition, place of introspection, place of looking-within-the-darkness, place of death and rebirth, place of transformation, place of the woman inside each of us, we give thanks for your power. Home of the bear who hibernates in winter, place of the snake who sheds its old skin and becomes dormant in winter, place of the unseen wolf, place of magic, symbolized by the deer, so graceful, even the larger bucks. Your color is black, and we give honor to the powers of the west, that we each may look within and find the richness inside us. Powers of the west, come in to guide and be with us now. And now, in silence, add a personal prayer to the west as you place your west crystal down in its place on your sacred wheel.

Powers of the north, place of work, place of the give-away, of sharing what one has learned, place of winter storms and the ability to survive them, hear our prayers. North, whose color is white, home of the buffalo, who gave away everything, each part of his body was used by the Indians, home of the bighorn sheep, the king of the desert, who can travel miles and miles without water. Place of strong winds, place of steep mountains, place of challenge, place of wisdom and intellect, powers of the north come in to guide and be with us now. And, in silence, now add your personal prayer to the north as you place your north crystal down on your sacred wheel.

Now sit in the center of your sacred wheel. Face east. As you think once again of the powers of the east, creativity, illumination, birth, sunrise, new life, I want you to focus your attention on the crystal of the east. Send energy out from your shaman center, the center of your being, right below your navel, out to the crystal. Then see that energy as golden light forming a bridge that reaches from your navel up into the sky. At the same time, call in an animal helper from the east to come and be with you. This may be any animal or bird. This is your helper from the east. The help you require from the east may be very different from the eagle or hawk that traditionally symbolizes the east. So now call in your animal spirit helper from the east. Your animal helper will come down the path of golden light. Take a few minutes in silence to let the animal come in. When your animal comes, welcome the animal. Offer some tobacco and cornmeal that you will find at the bottom of the pouch that is still on your side. Pause. Your animal has come to give you a message, to begin what can be a long journey, a lifetime journey of sharing knowledge. Ask your animal what message it has brought. The animal will give you a message about you and the power of the east, a message of help and guidance. Remember, in the Dreamtime, we communicate easily. Take silent time to commune with your animal, your spirit guide to the powers of the east, and to listen to its message.

Now give thanks to your east animal and let it know that you will contact it through using your crystals of the four directions in the future. Give thanks and say good-bye for now to your animal of the east.

Now turn and face south in your sacred circle. As you think once again of the powers of the south, place of trust and innocence, home of childlike wonder, place of taking one step at a time in balance and harmony, I want you to place your attention on the crystal of the south. Send energy out from your shaman center, the center of your being, right below your navel, out to the crystal. Then see that energy as ruby red light forming a shining bridge of light to the sky. As you focus your energy, call in an animal guide from the south to come down the bridge of light and work with you. This may be any animal or bird. This will be your helper from the south. Trust that the animal you need to help you develop your powers of the south will come. Now offer tobacco as you sit in your circle and take a few minutes in silence to let your animal spirit come in. Remember that even the mouse and squirrel, small and seemingly inconsequential creatures, have their own great powers in the sacred world. Now enter the silence and bring your animal in. If you "find" no animal, use your imagination and pick an animal to be with you. Remember, you must demand what you want in the spirit world. Pause.

Your animal from the south has come to give you a message. It has come to begin a relationship with you that can continue for a lifetime. Your animal of the south will teach you things you need to know about trust and innocence. Listen and dialogue now. Listen in the silence and remember what the animal of the south has to teach.

Now give thanks to your south animal. As you say good-bye, let it know you will contact it through using your four directions crystals in the future. Give thanks.

Now turn and face west in your sacred circle. As you think of the powers of the west, introspection, quiet, looking-within, place of dreams, place of the woman inside all of us, place your attention on your shaman center and also focus energy on the crystal of the west. Send energy out from the center of your being to the crystal. As you focus your energy, see your energy as brilliant black light forming a bridge to the sky. Call in an animal guide from the west to come down the beam of black light and be with you. This may be a bear, snake, deer, some traditional animals of the west, or it may be any animal or bird that you might require in order to learn more about your powers of the west. Now offer tobacco as you sit in your sacred circle and take a few minutes in silence to let your animal helper come in. Your animal will come to bring you a message about the power of the west.

Now give thanks to your spirit helper of the west and let it know that you will contact it through using crystals of the four directions in the future. Give thanks and say good-bye, for now, to your animal helper of the west.

Still relaxed and breathing easily, very centered, now turn in your sacred circle and face the north. Send energy out from your center, connecting with the crystal of the north. Begin to think of the powers of the north, home of wisdom, of work, of the man inside all of us, of giving away of our knowledge, place of storms and strong survival of storms. As you focus your energy and attention, see your energy as radiating white light forming a bridge to the sky and call in an animal guide from the north to come and work with you. This animal may be a buffalo or a bighorn ram, or it may be any animal or bird that you may require to learn what you need about the powers of the north.

Offer some tobacco and call in your animal now. See it come down the bridge of white light. Take a few minutes in silence to welcome your animal and to dialogue with it. Your spirit animal of the north has come to bring you a message to help you get in touch with your individual north power.

Take more time to see if there is anything else your spirit helper has to tell you at this time.

Now give thanks to your animal of the north, and let it know that you will contact it through using your crystals of the four directions in the future. Give thanks and say good-bye for now to your animal helper of the north.

Now as you sit in the center of your sacred wheel, once again let your breath be your focus. Let your breath drop down to the center of your being. Imagine the wind gently blowing your hair back. Your breath is like a gentle wind, changing you and lifting your energy, strengthening you and yet softening you. As you sit in the center of your circle, you will now see Agnes Whistling Elk, my teacher and your grandmother, approaching you. She is dressed in a Pendleton shirt of blue and red, has a turquoise necklace around her neck, wears a long denim skirt. Agnes has long grey braided hair. She is carrying a large folded blanket. As she walks, you are aware that she seems ancient; yet her face looks like she could be middle-aged. Agnes walks to the edge of your circle and places her blanket on the ground, spreading it out to reveal many objects on the blanket. She greets you by smiling and placing her two hands over her heart. Feel, imagine, visualize the warmth that emanates between the two of you. You and Agnes both feel welcomed.

On the blanket that Agnes has brought are many objects. These are tools of a warrior and warrioress. You are aware first of the many bright colors. Agnes will hold up the tools one by one, then pass them to you in order for you to become familiar with them.

First there is a painted shield. The shield is beautiful; it looks like old hide has been used. There is the profile of a horse in black on the brown hide, and above the horse's head are many yellow stars. Feel how your body feels when Agnes hands you the shield. There are five eagle feathers hanging from its rim.

Then, there is a small drum about a foot in diameter. You take the stick and beat the drum, noticing the way the drum sound reverberates throughout your body. There are red and yellow symbols for thunder and lightning painted on both sides of the drum.

Now there is a shining black obsidian blade with a handle made of elk horn. The blade is expertly chipped. The blade is four inches long and is tied to the elk horn with sinew. There is an oppressive strength that pours into your hands as you hold the blade. Feel this strength.

Agnes hands you a large five-foot lance that is made out of carved wood and is dressed with beads wrapped around it and also eight or ten large eagle feathers. The lance has an obsidian spearpoint at the tip. As you hold the lance, you feel like this lance is used more for ceremonial purposes. Notice whatever feelings move through your body.

Next Agnes carefully holds up and gives you a sacred personal pipe. The bowl is of red pipestone, very simply designed, a small elbow-shaped pipebowl. The long stem is wrapped in rabbit skin to symbolize the fertility of your spirit. Hold the pipe solidly in your hands. Allow your breath to guide your feelings.

Next there is a stone axe that looks like the most ancient tool of all. The stone is grey, solid, powerful, and the axe handle is completely wrapped in beads. You know that Agnes herself has wrapped the beads. She smiles as if sensing your thoughts. Allow yourself to feel whatever you feel as you hold the stone axe, possibly imagining those who have used the axe before. Then place the axe next to the other tools before you in your circle.

Next Agnes hands you a long bow and a quiver full of arrows. The arrows are painted with bright bands of color, as is the wonderfully bent bow. The arrowheads are meticulously chipped, elegant in themselves. The quiver is beaded in triangular and circular designs. You think of mountains and the wholeness of Mother Earth when you see these.

Now all these warrior's tools lie before you. And in the silence, Agnes has a message for you about your spirit self, your true warrior or warrioress nature. Listen now to Agnes's message to you. Take a moment.

Now we will once again move around the four directions of the sacred wheel to help you develop your talents and capacities in all the sacred directions. Ask yourself what your visionary, creative self of the east needs, which warrior's tool will help guide you in your journey to wholeness in the east. Listen in the silence. Shield, drum, obsidian blade, stone axe, lance, sacred pipe, bow and arrow—place whichever tool you need next to your crystal in the east, knowing that your east tool will help you throughout your life to develop your gifts of the east. Take a moment.

Which sacred warrior's tool—painted shield, drum, obsidian blade, stone axe, lance, sacred pipe, or bow and arrow—do you need to help you develop your gifts of trust and innocence, your childlike nature in the south? Choose your tool, place it at your south crystal, and in the silence listen for a message, information to come, to emanate from the tool, giving you a beginning teaching of how it will help you develp your south gifts of trust and innocence. Pause.

Now ask yourself which sacred tool—painted shield, drum, obsidian blade, stone axe, lance, pipe, or bow and arrow—you need to help you develop your gifts of intuition, of looking-within, of dreaming in the west. Choose your tool, and place it at your west crystal, and in the silence listen for a message, giving you a beginning teaching of how this tool will help you develp your west gifts of introspection and intuition. Pause.

Now ask yourself what tool you need in your north place, place of work, of sharing and giving away, place of wisdom. Do you need drum, painted shield, stone axe, lance, sacred pipe, painted shield, or bow and arrow in the place of the north? Listen in the silence, and place your chosen warrior's tool at your north crystal, listening for a message as to how this tool will help you begin to develop your gifts of wisdom, work, and teaching what you have learned. Pause.

Now you have a sacred warrior's tool and a power animal to help and guide you, protect and teach you in every direction. You are not alone in the Dreamtime, in the world of spirit and beauty. Walk clockwise around your circle. Go to all four directions: east, south, west, and north. See your animals and your warrior's tools in each direction. You now have your council to discuss problems with and your weapons to fight with in the war against ignorance. Use them well. Say a prayer of thanks at each place and return to the center of your wheel. Take a number of minutes in silence to do this. We can never give enough thanks, enough prayers of thanksgiving.

Now once again as you stand in the center of your wheel, see Agnes Whistling Elk come out from the trees she had retreated into.

With your permission, she will enter your circle. She enters from the east and offers cornmeal at each direction and in the center. You welcome her and her blessing. Agnes faces you and you hug. You feel Agnes's hair as you wrap your arms around her back, feel her Pendleton shirt, feel also her turquoise stone necklace gently pressing into your chest. She smells of cedar and the north wind. You feel as if she is giving you something; then you realize that you are both giving something. You are exchanging love, one human being to another. The beauty of this hug, you feel, is more durable than many exchanges of affection. This hug feels as if it will last forever. With that knowledge, you and Agnes separate, knowing you have joined in a way in which somehow you will always be together. You both nod and smile, and Agnes leaves your sacred wheel from the east, her eyes serene and glowing. You feel filled with radiant light. Agnes turns and points to the crystal that still rests on your chest. A beam of golden, white light emanates from her finger and illuminates your crystal as she slowly disappears. Physically take hold of your crystal and place it on your shaman eye—your third eye. See the crystal becoming filled with golden, white light as it vibrates at a higher and more intense rate. Your entire body begins to tingle with the increased rate of vibration. You begin to feel a oneness with the crystal as you harmonize exactly with its vibration.

Take a deep breath, and gently move your consciousness into the crystal by merging the luminosity of your body with the golden, white light of the crystal. Move around inside the crystal and experience the crystalline beauty, prismatic colors, purple, green, white—rainbows. Feel all your *chakras* opening and vibrating with power and light. Become the light for a moment. Experience the spires of crystal formations like ice and the bubbles of perfection within them. Inside the crystal there is great clarity. Explore and find a place of power, a special place that is yours within the crystal. Sit down and place a red medicine blanket and all your sacred, precious things in front of you. See a beam of sunlight coming in from the top of the crystal. It forms a bridge of light reaching from the heavens into the crystal. Sing your power song to yourself and roll your eyes up. Then see your medicine woman, whoever she may be, walking down the beam of rainbow light to the blanket. Take your time as you begin to see her more clearly. When she reaches you, stand up and give each other a hug. She has a gift for you.

Take it and hold it to your heart. Then give her your gift. Remember how this exchange makes you feel. Then touch a crystal to her third eye. Feel her essence. Then hold the crystal to your own third eye.

Sense the love and communion that passes between you. Know that you can ask her anything. She is your teacher. See a silver chord of light like a laser connecting her heart to yours. Feel connection, love, and trust. Know that you can always go into this crystal as you have just done and consult with her on any matter. Do this often. Before she leaves, visualize yourself sitting in your sacred wheel. See your power animal and your medicine woman sitting with you, surrounded by your animal helpers and your tools. Then see the little people, the Goowawas, smiling and sitting around your circle, with the dingo and Oruncha of Chauritzi standing with Agnes Whistling Elk as they exchange a beautiful crystal. Focus on your heart center and remember the power of these beings who are your new family. Feel the crystals live with vision inside you. Commune for a moment with each of them. Then let this vision fade.

Then say good-bye for now, and see your medicine woman walk back up that rainbow beam of light until she disappears. Roll up your blanket and sacred things, and leave them in the crystal on your power spot.

Move your essence like light out of your crystal until you experience being back on the floor. Hold the crystal to your third eye, and give thanks to the Great Spirit for bringing you your teacher and medicine woman. Then blow your breath into the crystal in your hand, and slowly open your eyes as you feel comfortable doing so.

WORKSHEET

Describe your weapons, each and every one, and which directions you put them in. Also describe your power animals and each of the directions you put them in.

South

West

North

East

How did Agnes Whistling Elk appear to you? What emotions were
brought up as you saw her and greeted her?

Describe any other tools that you felt you needed that Agnes did not bring to you. Describe why you needed them and of what use they would have been to you.

What is the name of your medicine woman?

Describe her hair, her clothes, etc.

What was her gift for you? Describe it. How did it make you feel?

What was your gift to her? Describe it.

You are my backbone and you are my life,
  Mother Earth,
and I will bring harmony to your land. Ho!
                    —Twin Dreamers

Chapter 12

The Knot Ceremony

Introduction

These meditations and visualizations have been a gift from Agnes Whistling Elk, Ruby Plenty Chiefs, the Sisterhood, and myself to aid you on your journey to enlightenment into your shaman path.

This knot ceremony has always been done at the end of a meeting of the Sisterhood, and it has been done with many other groups in the world to show the oneness we all experience with the universe, with the stars, with all that lives. It is to exemplify that we are indeed all a circle and that our dreams and prayers are at the core of this circle. If you are doing this work in a group, it helps to put a prayer into something that is tangible, something you can take away from the circle that reminds you of your work and your growth together. If you are working alone, it is still important to tie a knot and place a prayer within that knot. Cut the cord away, take that knot, and put it in your medicine bag. That knot will be with you forever to remind you of your place in the stars.

We are made from stars and to the stars we must one day return.

Ceremony

Pass pieces of twine around if you are in a group. The length of this twine will represent your circle. As I said at the beginning of our work together, we are a circle, and our lives, our dreams, our work, our power are intermixed. This circle that we make will send its harmony out into the universe, and we each shall carry the responsibility to create beauty and healing with our lives, to symbolize the continuation of this circle, for I do believe that your circle will continue even if some of you never see each other again if you are working in a group. We are in each other's hearts.

So with this in mind, pass the twine around. Each person takes the twine, unwieldy as it may be, and ties a knot in it. As you tie the knot, I would like you to say a prayer, a silent prayer for yourself. Each of you has an individual prayer, a prayer for your lives, for your hearts, for healing; and I would like you to add your individual prayer to the universal circle of sacred consciousness.

We are all a circle. Our dreams and prayers are at their core, the same dreams and prayers. Your circle will lead out into the world and spread harmony over many parts of this earth. To remind you of this circle, cut out one knot. This knot will bind you together in higher circles, each of us responsible for one other person's prayer, responsible for each other's prayers, and the prayer that your circle represents.

Offer your knot up to the Great Spirit. We are now separate and we are now joined. May our prayers be as one. May our unique spirits thrive individually and together.

Ho!

Epilogue

Now that you have worked through these meditations and visualizations, I would like you to write down a short story about yourself. At this point, you should have gotten very in touch with your life, with what you need to give up to proceed up the mountain of your evolvement. Somewhere at the root of all of our lives is a wound. In society, we tend to shy away from this wound, to cover it up, to put a bandage over it and forget that we are indeed in this earth walk to become enlightened. In the seeds of our discontent, of our wound, of our pain is great knowledge. The source of our pain is actually the source of our enlightenment. Therefore, I would like you to describe what you consider your wound in life, your greatest wound, and write a story around that pain about how you feel you came onto this earth to experience this pain and how you are going to heal it. What do you need to find within the shaman path to heal this wound within you? This story can be as long as you want or as short as you want, but I want it to be from the depths of your being. I need you to keep this story because in our second phase of work, in the intermediate development of your shaman path, which I will be working with you on, hopefully, in the future, I need you to bring this story to me. I need to work on it with you. So craft it carefully, think about it, spend some days in meditation now that you have gone through the teachings around the sacred wheel.

Before you begin this story, I want you to go out and find a powerful tree, a grandmother or a grandfather tree. I want you to sit with your back to it and meditate for several hours about this whole process that you have just been through. Finally, come to that still place within you where you feel the wound and the pain that you need to give away. If you feel that you have actually dealt with that wound completely and that it is gone from your life, then write about that and how you have come to this place of peace within you.

I thank you for your effort and your attention and your energy. Please join me in this prayer from my heart to yours:

Great Spirit whose voice we hear in the winds and the trees, Mother Earth whose breath gives us life, help us to walk in beauty and strength and to learn the lessons that are hidden in the stones and the trees and the waters of the sea. Give us strength to fight out greatest enemy, ignorance. Great Spirit, hear the sounds of our grateful hearts, and help us to find the wisdom and joy and power that is locked within each of our souls. We are the reflections of you, Great . Spirit. Join us on our path as we join you for all the days of our lives. Ho!

In Spirit and Love,
Lynn Andrews

WORKSHEET

Your Story

For the last ten years, I've been describing my learning and my path. It has been a joy to do this. In continuing my journey, I would be grateful if you would share your insights with me.

Please write me at this address:

> Lynn Andrews
> 2934½ Beverly Glen Circle
> Box 378
> Los Angeles, CA 90077

Send me your name and address so I can share any new information with you.